OFFLINE

D0063193

The Less-Digital Guide
to Creative Work

BY JESS HENDERSON

MATTERS

BIS PUBLISHERS
Building Het Sieraad
Postjesweg 1
1057 DT Amsterdam
The Netherlands

+31 (0)20 515 02 30
bis@bispublishers.com
www.bispublishers.com

ISBN 978 90 6369 578 1

Copyright © 2020 L. Henderson and BIS Publishers.
Copy Editor: Luke Munn
With thanks to Hannah Cheney, Ana Joldes and Sean Peron.
Thank you to Yumna Al-Arashi for the beautiful photo.

ACKNOWLEDGEMENTS

This is for all the readers of Outsider and for all fellow outsiders on the inside. Thank you for your generous and critical guidance.

Thank you to my mother, my brother, my sunshine, and the wise man who changed my life in 2019.

And a big thank you to Joachim Baan and Jordi Carles for their stunning design. This book wouldn't be what it is without you.

PREFACE

*Hope locates itself in the premises that we don't know
what will happen and that in the spaciousness of uncertainty
is room to act.*   REBECCA SOLNIT

I have woven a parachute out of everything broken.
                                            WILLIAM STAFFORD

I finished the final manuscript of this book the week the Covid-19 virus was announced as a pandemic. The question of *to lock down or not to lock down* lingered in Europe for a couple of weeks before we started retreating into our homes and leaning on our technologies harder than ever. Two camps emerged: those who saw the window as the long-awaited permission to slow, and those who hyped up the hyper-connection in order to cope.

The drive to continue work or study quickly engulfed much of the first encampment. Days became full of video calls – sometimes with clients or colleagues, sometimes with friends and family, and sometimes with that unique extra group: those whom we had lost touch with in the haste of *before*. Our phones became our life lines and we found comfort from the same lights, sounds, and notifications that were oppressing us just weeks earlier – until the oppression came back around, harder and more disorienting than ever. As one student from Rome wrote: 'Allegedly, this virus has robbed people of their social life due to social distancing, but did it, really? The truth is that social physical interaction was robbed by social media way before the Coronavirus even existed... The majority of us now use this calamity as an excuse for our excessive social media use'. Compared with socialising face-to-face, a life where 'connection' came purely through incoming notifications and ongoing Zoom calls felt like a deprived substitute.

My dear friend Dalia told me 'we need to become friends with the virus', and I saw it was doing much of the work this book set out to do. It reminded us that the quieter camp is there. It provided an opening, an opportunity. And it suggested a form of creative work that was less dictated by – and worshipping of – digital 'solutions'. People began valuing the physical interactions that were taken for granted before and had now become punishable. Walks outside, physical hang outs, films watched in cinemas, and the freedom to come and go in the world as you please – all these unconscious acts now became precious. They gained a scary past-like quality, relics from a time before. Sure, we lost our freelance jobs but we can recognise that we gained a lot too. I'm bound to this small apartment with my buddy who happens to be my romantic partner. It's a special situation for a couple; we are getting to know each other in ways previously unknown, we have the time and (lack of) space to care for each other that we didn't have in the busyness of life before. We may look back on this time as some of the seminal days of our togethered-lives.

I am fully aware that we are experiencing this from a position of privilege. Some will be experiencing today with immense pain, insecurity, and loneliness. Some will not be able to recover from a hard day of isolation with a hug. Physical contact assures me that offline matters. The rustling of the leaves, walking a street, the way a stranger's smile from behind a mask touches me deeply – these meaningful occurrences highlight the key role that offline plays in an increasingly virtual world.

We continue to look forward, forward, forward, and once the dust settles, we know that things will not look the same again. We will use our ad-hoc skills and knowledge to develop new tendencies where having so much will become bad taste and being resourceful will become second nature. That means ideas, imagination and creativity – not beautiful bags, bright white sneakers, bought experiences, and *who is the busiest*-statuses – will reign supreme. The unanswered questions of 'how to implement the changes we desire?', the same questions posed in this book, have answers that are becoming clearer. One comrade noted during their lockdown experience that 'Online is a nightmare. Online is you, the screen, and then you and the screen again. And your friends and colleagues imprisoned in little small cells inside it, as if they were kids' puppets popping out of the puppet theatre'. We will remember what it was like to have the physical presence of each other removed, and we will remember how our online substitutes fell desperately short.

This moment is an opportunity to deconstruct and reconstruct our digital habitats. A new start that shifts from reformist to radical is now central to the conversation. What feels 'fair' is changing. As power relations are unveiled and come under examination, the strategies for resistance will change too. I hope we can remember the power that comes from the inside, and that it is the masses of precarious workers (freelance creatives, and delivery workers alike) that are revealing the flaws long embedded in the system, and all the inhumanity and fragility that comes with it.

Dare we say it – did you slightly enjoy the time at home in between the bouts of confusion and despair? Did you learn new things, gain new perspectives on meaning, make with your hands, revisit lost connections, and find a focus you thought was long gone? Did you get a fresh healthier relationship with your devices? We all saw a lot of creative thinking being born, and a lot of deeper distraction ensue. I learnt that when you have a deep connection to yourself, others, and nature, it becomes a lot less necessary to find fulfilment in a screen.

We have new experiences and new knowledge to go forth with. What are we going to do with them? Rebecca Solnit relays how, in the wake of Hurricane Katrina, people 'had talent for valuing other things more than productivity and efficiency, the miserable virtues that hustle people past each other and everyday attentiveness and pleasure'. We've switched from being good consumers and bad citizens to bad consumers and good citizens. 'Consumers are Creators' was the old trope. Not anymore. Mutual aid, empathy, volunteerism, friendship, solidarity, and support are all here. Our period of economic un-growth is leading to greater inner and social growth. We are getting smarter at using our time and smarter at making a living – in the fullest sense of the word.

What's next in our world of unknowns? I want to find out in physical company, as well as with those friends who are far away. It's the future dance of being together with other bodies and together with online affordances. It's an unprecedented time. Take a moment. Think about what you want more of. What you want less of. Offline is a possibility space. Perhaps now more than ever. Take seriously the opportunity to remake. It's a once in a lifetime experience, in more ways than one.

WELCOME

Is it just me or is it getting crazier out there?   JOKER

Words from the 2019 film of the same name that we could utter ourselves from behind the not-so-safety of our laptop screens. Why do we find ourselves in unwavering devotion to the online when we know how much offline matters?

Throughout my career as a 'creative professional' (or is it 'professional creative'?) I've been asking myself this. I was 18 when it began. A full ten years have passed since, and yet that same question still haunts me every day. A feeling that a swift current was carrying us away from a vital element of life. Offline. Anything. Not as a romanticised past, momentary detox, or place we are banished to for digital overuse. But as a space of possibility. As quickly as the current was moving, the 'creativity' in creative work was drying up. Peers took pride in identifying as 'creatives'. I didn't feel proud. It was boring. Everything revolved around social media, gaming 'engagement' metrics, and trying to think hard about 'immersive digital experiences'. Doing things face-to-face, getting people together, being experimental or weird – all that faded. Dismissed as ineffective. If data isn't showing it is a trend, it is not allowed. At best an alternative idea might be humoured with 'prove it works'. If you can't produce numbers upfront and guarantee a return on investment, there is no way the idea will live. Fun is now forbidden. Creativity-as-work is a serious business. The 'digital-first' mindset has become doctrine.[§] To suggest anything else is seen as sabotaging the task at hand. Meanwhile, that all-knowing 'data' still goes unquestioned. At both business and personal levels, there is zero criticism and zero discomfort about its collection or use.

The statement 'prove it' encapsulates the essence of creativity-as-work today. Ideas need quantifiable results. 'Prove it' lives on with its brother question 'does it work?', an enduring classic you're sure to meet if you start to experiment with the offline. What is this question asking? What does 'work' mean here? Is it code for 'make money'? What is the answer we want to hear? My suspicion would be that it's something like this: 'Yes, it's a surefire way to make money, we have the numbers that say so'. But what about the negative side of this equation? Does it still 'work' when the work itself, the worker, and the audience all suffer as a result?

'DIGITAL-FIRST', ALSO KNOWN AS 'DIGITAL BY DEFAULT', IS AN APPROACH THAT
PRIORITISES RELEASING CONTENT INTO DIGITAL AND ONLINE COMMUNICATION CHAN-
NELS OVER 'TRADITIONAL MEDIA'. THIS MEANS ORIENTING INFORMATION TO THE
INTERNET RATHER THAN OFFLINE PLACES SUCH AS PRINT MEDIA, REAL LIFE EVENTS
OR BILLBOARDS. WITH THE 'DIGITAL-FIRST' DISTRIBUTION OF CONTENT, NEW PRAC-
TICES HAVE BEEN INTRODUCED, INCLUDING THE COLLECTION, USE, AND MANAGEMENT
OF DATA, WHICH TRACKS READERSHIP, AND DEPENDENCE AND COMPLIANCE WITH THE
ONLINE ADVERTISING DUOPOLY (GOOGLE AND FACEBOOK).

§

Here we should pay attention to that nagging feeling, to our intuitions and suspicions. Regardless of whether or not we have the numbers or the words to explain it, we can sense that the eradication of offline interactions is having an undesirable impact. Feelings are real. Feelings are significant. This is proof that must not be ignored. There are external confirmations and reports, studies and surveys, but ultimately our innate knowledge is screaming loud enough. We don't need hard numbers to confirm it. There is an ever-growing sense pointing us to the value of getting together or taking time out offline – both for ourselves and for the creative in our work. Output included.

In this setting, what was supposedly creative work has become dull, repetitive, and misguided. 'It's all happening online now!' they insist – 'they' being everyone from the bosses in our offices to the marketing futurists and platforms themselves. In-real-life has become passé. Ideas are now based on the results of algorithms and Best Practice Guides. The word 'creativity' itself has been tainted by an industry that stole it for a name. They have drained it of meaning and drained us – the workers at the front lines – of energy and criticality. Today's 'creative' industries more closely resemble a factory for online advertising with a sociopathic tendency for consumerism and greed. Once inside this machine, it doesn't take long for the unavoidable question to arise: 'What is it we are creating?'

As we creative workers toil, my brother sits at university being groomed to enter the creativity-as-work scene. The university presents this site of work as aspirational while paradoxically preparing students for little more than exploitation. Students prep their CVs for unpaid internships, implicitly told that 'doing what you love' should be adequate remuneration. 'Stay hungry, stay foolish' said Steve Jobs to students in his Stanford University commencement speech. Did he mean forever?

OUTSIDER TURNED INSIDER

For three years I have been documenting the dwindling consideration for offline alternatives in creative work. It began in a moment of frustration after sitting at the table of yet another 'social media strategy' pitch at the creative agency I was working at. I was over being the token millennial at the table. I was sick of hearing the well-worn query: 'How do we reach a younger target audience?' only to have the predictable Social Media Solution proposed once more. I got déjà vu watching this room discuss the behaviour of 'youth today' with baseless conviction. I went back to my desk and wrote a no-bullshit critique of social media becoming the answer to every question – often before a question has even been asked. This is especially true for anything to do with the young or anything to do with 'connection' and 'community'. The piece was probing at these automatic behaviours while beginning to think seriously about offline. The ever-expanding concept yet shrinking reality of the offline space. This small treatise was sent under the pseudonym of Jess from Outsider to everyone I knew in these lines of work.

From there, Outsider became a weekly email newsletter. What started with a readership of 50 quickly took on a life of its own, and was soon being sent to the inboxes of over 5000 people. In fact, the existence of this book is a direct response to their requests. That weekly newsletter built a shelter for fellow workers of the cultural industries suffering the same daily challenges under the tyranny of online obsession. This Cult of the Digital takes over everything, from ruining the work itself to depleting the physical and psychic selves of those making it. It is no coincidence that the rise of this 'tech-determinism' in creative work coincides with increased personal exhaustion, device-related anxieties, and the overall dissolution of explosive, challenging creativity. We need to be radically aware that creative work is overly emphasising digital solutions to our detriment. Fads come and go (TikTok! VR experiences! Podcasts!) but the mythology surrounding the efficacy of the digital remains.

ARRIVING HERE: OUR JUMP-OFF POINT

The presence of 'digital-first' motivations influence our work in more ways than one. From the type of creation to overwork culture and the rise of risk aversion, it's all connected. These are the constellation of topics that surround the offline, in relation to creative work. Let's poke fun at the situation while also poking at the problems. This book hopes to take you on a trip through an unusual variety of elements: approaches, realities, delusions, possibilities.

Today a quick-fix solution is what books are expected to provide. Something tidy and easy. This is not that book. It isn't a clean list of offline tips and tricks. It's a provocation based on the feeling that something isn't right. That something can be different. We're not here for the clickbait reduction of nonconformist ideas. Leave mainstream expectations at the door. This is a radically honest take on what's happening and what might be done.

These thoughts are informed by my experience working as a strategist in agencies and the in-house marketing departments of fashion brands and cultural organisations. If not identical to your situation, I still hope you will find a commonality, something that resonates with you. This book relates to the general experience of making a living from creative work, whether you're a senior art director or an intern. When it comes to ideas or exploitation – usually both ends of the spectrum are included. These environments are commercial. Tech, design, and advertising are highly fluid, now virtually indistinguishable. To deny this (for instance, pretending a creative agency is not just a nicer name for marketing or advertising agency) is unnecessary. Most, if not all, creative work is marketing in some shape or form. Whether you're an illustrator hired by a culinary service to draw cooking tools or a museum director building a programme to attract visitors – it's all marketing. Within this setting, I document problems and contemplate opportunities to take a different approach. This thinking combines two strands: our personal dislike with being advertised to and a sense that the very output we're making can surely improve. I strive to address the people commissioning this work as much as those making it. A constant advertising landscape is the situation we live in. It forms our surroundings. If you spend any time online, it's the infrastructure of almost the entire landscape. Online is transactions. The offline too. There are other transactions than advertising. This is what we are here to address – what can be done right here, right now?

I want something better than a life tethered to consumer culture. As both creator and audience, we get the full spectrum fallout of negative advertising, from smart phone distractions and ongoing burnouts,[‡1] to scary surveillance, privacy breaches, and irritating algorithm holes. These are the thrills and disturbances of the accelerated, hyper-stimulating culture of today, one that now feels as intolerable as it does overwhelming. We are all constant victims of invasive online marketing. And we have all been that person at that table, watching another done-to-death digital 'concept' being suggested, looking around the room feeling crazy, unable to believe that we're the only one thinking: 'Is this the best we've got?'

When Outsider first began, it was a personal vehicle to escape that shrinking horizon of possibility. Going to work meant facing maddening complacency. Life's main prospect seemed to be an impoverished creativity – for both my own life and those on the receiving end of this marketing drivel. As creative workers we find ourselves oddly suspended, being both the creator and the target of this commercial output. In sharing these dreams and grievances, the newsletter became an unforeseen way of connecting with like minds. Not only did I write to these listening bodies, but they wrote to me. Subverting the traditional push-only format, we soon forged a solidarity that didn't have nor need a face. I could write as a no-holds-barred, cold-shower-giving comrade, while also providing a warm hearted confirmation that what you're feeling is real and you are not alone. Outsider was a home for thinking about offline as a space for doing things differently. This was not a romanticised lifestyle, not a return to typewriters and flip-phones. Instead, I wanted to explore an offline life that looked forward. As an antidote. As a potential. Not as a quick refresh then back to work, more productive than before. Rather than anti-technology, this was pro-human contentment, pro-oddity, and pro-enjoyment of life.

That place for Outsiders has become this book that you hold in your hands. This is for anybody seeking strategies that are counter-cultural to the all-digital-everything delusion that clouds creative work today. It's for anybody wondering why we are not getting together, in the face of being driven apart. From old hands to new grads, those on the brand side or those fulfilling the briefs sent out, this book is for all involved in the world of creativity-as-work. In all its shapes and forms. None of us need more wealthy ad-men telling us how to fail better. Instead we need fun, wit, and trojan horse-thinking.

You hold in your hands a compendium of strategies and alternative creativity acts that understands and subverts business as usual. A human-first approach in a digital-first world. Not only applicable to how we make a living, but how to live at large. A guide for how to engage radically with life. This book wants to rouse us out of our complacency and into critical thinking. I long for a rise of giving-a-shit, a refusal to let this situation go unchallenged. But this fiery provocation is tempered with the lightness to let it all go for the things that matter most, like human connections and hanging out. This is about changing the face of work by acknowledging there is more to life than work. We need to return joy to the everyday, meet up, and resist individual retreats. Embrace absurdity. Bring on a weird creativity that acts socially and cares more about quality of life than it does for selling stuff. Here's a vote for bringing offline from the fringe into the centre. This is your wild trip through provocative non-conformity. It made it into your hands for a reason. You're ready for a wake-up. You're ready to do things differently.

PART
ONE:
REALITY

Doesn't anybody notice this?
I feel like I'm taking crazy pills!   MUGATU

Have you ever felt like Will Ferrell's character Mugatu in
Zoolander? Mugatu watches as the world worships Derek Zoolander's
modelling, reacting as though his every move is original and varied.
In reality, far from being a talented chameleon, Zoolander looks
identical in every shot and situation. Eventually Mugatu explodes at the
emperor's-new-clothes level of insanity – how is everyone going along
with this? Am I the only one seeing what's going on? These questions
could be our own. Sometimes working in the field of creativity feels
like taking crazy pills.

We look around and wonder how so much can be so off, and yet
the prevailing attitude is blind or blasé. The consideration for anything
not online has been quickly diminished, with an array of strange
realities left in its wake. Let's blow these wide open.

IT'S   ALL   MARKETING
Recognising   Reality
and   Living   with   Ourselves

Being contrarian towards classical advertising is easy for creative workers. Clearly our work is above that.

'I'm curating line-ups for festivals'.

'I'm defining the visual language'.

'I'm guiding the gallery's publishing arm'.

'I'm Head of Communication'.

*'I'm not living in Mad Men,
this is cultural material we're making here'.*

Let's get real, it's all marketing.

Marketing is the bedrock of the business, the cornerstone to making a living from 'creative' pursuits. Its twin directives of appeal (cool job) and return (making a living) may take infinite shapes and forms, some more subtle than others, but they are always there. The recognition of this is often painful as it touches on the deep horror of 'selling out', a verdict that we are quick to give, but slow to suspect of ourselves. We identify as being artists, not advertisers.

EVERYTHING IS MARKETING

Everything is marketing, but creative labour will continue to masquerade as anything other than this. After all, this skit is necessary to convince creators that their art deserves to be underpaid, that their expectations should remain low, and that they should be grateful for any job they can get. Recognising 'everything is marketing' is the first step to seeing through this charade. Not only are we selling out, we're buying in. George Monbiot tackles this discomfort in a piece for the Guardian aptly titled *Sucking Out Our Brains Through Our Eyes: Advertising trashes our happiness and trashes the planet. And my income depends on it.* In its final paragraph the writer acknowledges:

I detest this poison, but I also recognise that I am becoming more dependent on it. As sales of print editions decline, newspapers lean even more heavily on advertising. Nor is the problem confined to the commercial media. Even those who write only for their own websites rely on search engines, platforms, and programmes ultimately funded by advertising. We're hooked on a drug that is destroying society.

Like a form of class anxiety, we would prefer to fall under the much critiqued 'Creative Class' than anything associated with the square suits-and-ties world of advertising. Despite disliking advertising's 'normie' *non-cultural* reputation, there may be a form of acknowledgement that this denial is missing out on. I don't mean the social acceptance of their 'real job', I mean the financial recognition that creative work so commonly lacks. Perhaps if we were not afraid to attach our work to marketing, the work we do would be elevated to the same category as those with explicit Marketing or Advertising titles, and thus deserving of higher remuneration. Instead, we settle for empty but cooler-sounding titles, a false sense of greater moral good from our work, and social 'cred' as pay.

Reflecting on her time working in Silicon Valley, former tech worker Anna Weiner describes a similar situation:

At the beginning, I bought into the industry's stories about itself: its exceptionalism and moral superiority, its vision for a new and better world. I thought the industry was the future, and it felt really good to participate. After a while, though, this mentality started to show fault lines. I had a lot of questions and qualms about the endgame. Core values started to seem really pernicious. The idea that your economic output is equal to your value as a person, or to your value in society, is both pervasive and dangerous.[‡1]

So while we're quick to identify as artists or creatives before uttering 'ad agency', how do we live with the reality of 'it's all marketing' when it conjures such unease? Creativity has been co-opted and exploited as a means to sell products, fuel gentrification, and strengthen capitalism's pathologies – to name just a few of its achievements. As anarchist activist artist Cindy Milstein observes, 'Our rebellious ad busting has become indistinguishable from advertisements employing rebellion-as-sales-pitch… Without constant awareness, we almost unwittingly take up the project of this society of control, with its fragmentation, insecurity, and shallow infotainment'[2]. Despite these circumstances we find ourselves in, I still believe that transgressive thought and creative experimentation present a powerful way to heal societal dysfunctions and alter the future from our sometimes seemingly inexorable slide into dystopia. Even when it is a commercial deviation.

Does creativity refer only to different forms of an ever identical economic content?
Or does it mean the ability to imagine a world beyond the boundaries of the economic?[3] FRANCO 'BIFO' BERARDI

THREE STEPS TO LIVING WITH OURSELVES

1. DECONSTRUCT THE DENIAL THAT CREATIVE WORK IS NOT MARKETING.
    Marketing is an icky, archaic-sounding word, but to deny it may be doing more harm than good to our precarious situation. Marketing work is acknowledged as deserving fair pay, whereas 'creative work' is considered less deserving.

2. DIFFERENTIATE 'SELLING OUT' FROM SOLIDARITY
    We are all in the same boat, whether outright 'Brand Strategists' at ad agencies or freelance illustrators for cultural institutions. Forge solidarity and counter the competitiveness ingrained in creative labour.

3. DISBELIEVE THE MYTH THAT CREATIVITY AT WORK LEAVES NO SPACE FOR RADICALITY
    Infusing our output with critical thinking, new visions, and expansive transgressions opens up many more possibilities than it closes down. Scan for places where potency lies, get together, and start looking beyond the present. As Anna points out: 'I was able to stay sceptical but continue working by doing something that shouldn't have felt novel: I treated my job like a job'.

OFFLINE ACTION AND INACTION
A   New   Vision   of   Value

'OFFLINE'?

Offline is a mindset, a methodology, a possible approach, an alternative, a lens to put ideas through and see what comes out the other side. Offline is as abstract as it is tangible. It is a place we know and a state of being we recognise. It lives open to interpretation and evolves alongside technological developments. At one time, TV and radio were offline. Now they are not. Stickering a street is considered an offline action. And yet the urge to photograph this intervention and post it online can arise. The lines are not clean. Offline means stepping back from the urge of instant gratification. Offline is a possibility space that exists away from the internet.

Regardless of its current state of flux, we know the effects of looking each other in the eye, of exchanging smiles with a stranger, of making things with our hands, or of going a day without using our phones. We know how this feels and this feeling makes offline solid to experience. It gives us a grounding, assuring us that offline matters.

These sensations are as real and pressing as they are potent and instinctual. 'In real life', face-to-face, existence away from the infosphere gains importance every day. Its eradication from creative work and replacement with digital substitutes comes at a cost to the creativity itself. Dictated entirely by the 'findings', data-driven work becomes safe and dull. The negative impacts of these decisions take their toll on the lives of both makers and receivers. Anxiety, burnout, capitalism, consumerist culture, social media sadness, digital overwhelm, loneliness, depression, precarious creative labour, and the fading of offline considerations from all spheres of life – we all know this is a list of attributes that are deeply correlated.

If online indicates a state of connectivity to the network, then offline implies a disconnected state. 'The distinction between online and offline is conventionally seen as the distinction between computer-mediated communication and face-to-face communication, respectively'.[+1] Perhaps disconnected from the internet, though not disconnected from the reality that is non-virtual. *IRL*. In times past, online was also expressed as 'on the line'. Today this description seems more fitting than ever. To be connected to the network means putting yourself, your information, and your emotional wellbeing on the line. To take the equipment, subsystem, or self offline is to reconnect with what exists inside.

A device that is offline uses no external clock reference and relies upon its own internal clock.[+2]   BILL GIBSON

We are dreaming of offline. From no-WiFi cafés to digital detox weekends, raves with a 'leave your phone at the door' policy and best-seller books such as Cal Newport's *Digital Minimalism* – the Right to Disconnect is beginning to take shape and give shape to contemporary culture. There is more to this than a simple ethical idea of 'opting out'. Because 'opting out' is not so simple. It is increasingly difficult to do so. My bank, for instance, is removing the option of non-online banking. To get a discount at the petrol station, you need to have their mobile application. These examples show how our lives are entwined with digital connection. Beyond these practicalities, to 'disconnect' relates to our primary need for connection with others. It effects it. It can deny it.

Yet if there are promises here, there are also pitfalls. One risk is that offline becomes a space of guilt and self-punishment. A place we are banished to for spending 'too much time on the feeds'. Oddly, we often perceive it as being a penalty rather than a reward. It is not an immediate relief. There is pain. Offline has insufficient dopamine hits, withdrawals that can take too long to endure. It takes too long to make it through to the other side – to the promised land of pleasure, revival, and a reinstatement of who you used to be. And so, we go back online. Issues remain unresolved and the eternal cycle of emptiness resumes once more.

OFF OR ON?

Offline vs. online is not a binary decision. We are far past that. Offline is not a lifestyle. Offline is a demonstratively different line of thought. A different route for creative work to take. A different order of values and a different mode of behaviour. A condition that enables transformation. Offline is a possibility space. A clearing. A liminal and motile area. A vast expanse, potent in its vacancy. As Franco Berardi reminds us: 'Potency gives us the potential to be free and to transform the environment'.[‡3]

Now, more than ever, there is an urgent need to bring the offline back to the fore. It has been pushed to the fringes, incorrectly associated with primitivist 'off-the-grid' lifestyle attempts. Such 'unplug' retreats are but a brief recalibration before heading back to screen-oriented business as usual. This is not what we are talking about. 'Going offline' is unfairly advised as a reenergising tactic. After a few days off you're ready for another bout of overwork. Or even more painfully, prescribed as self-punishment for too much 'gramming. Offline as the connection-starved corner we are banished to. A space of guilt. DIY rehab for your email problem. These connotations of offline action (or inaction) result in a kind of dry denial when set against the excitement ability to make, live, and prioritise 'online'. Digital-first is the doctrine of creative work today, but we don't have to be one of its disciples. It is neither predetermined nor the only mode of operation. Nothing is inevitable. The majority of those who perpetuate the mythologies of a life and work deep in digital-everything don't know what they're doing. They are blinded by the fear of missing out. They don't care for the impacts and they don't know the options. They hear talk of 'offline' as an ill-informed waste of our digital future. Yet we're all aware of how online has become a problematic space we never asked for. Rather than staring at the narrowing horizon of this darkening future, offline beckons us with its alternative possibilities. Reconsidering what we treasure offline could even provide clues for improving our online practices and platforms.

Technology isn't inherently progressive.[‡4]
THE XENOFEMINIST MANIFESTO

The recentring of offline considerations is an application of energy beyond the here and now. It values people and our dynamism. Nothing about offline is nostalgic – it is entirely next. As Franco Berardi asserted, 'potency is the energy that transforms the possibilities into actualities'.[‡5] This area is ripe and ready. Offline is not anti-digital nor anti-development, but pro-improvement, pro-enthusiasm, and pro-collective flourishing. Offline is the fight for the internal space, the very notion of what it means to be human.

GET   A   LIFE
NOT   A   LIFESTYLE

STAYING CALM

In *Staying with the Trouble*, Donna Haraway states, in a beautiful and ironic way, that there are two reactions to technology today. 'On one side, there are the techno-optimists, who believe that technology will save humanity, the planet, and the environment. On the other side are the techno-apocalyptics, who say *no way, technology will destroy everything'*.[6]

Haraway takes a different stance, telling us to keep calm. She says that it isn't a tragedy that the human race is doomed to disappear. It's an inevitability that reminds us to let go a little. It suggests we recentre on the things we care about the most. Rather than our phones, those things are probably the people around us.

The importance of what we act upon and create offline cannot be underestimated. The atmosphere around it is inimitable. The impact on mental health, enthusiasm, collective joy, solidarity, connectivity – all of this – has value that cannot be explained in terms of money. Here is a value that accounts for people, moments, and intricacies weightier than the numbers on quarterly financial reports. If you shifted your efforts to breaking out into offline action, redirecting typed words into real life experience, what do you think would happen? An immediate distinction from the sea of sameness in creative work today, and an enhanced experience of life on both sides – that of the creator (you) and the receiver (us).

The mere knowledge of offline as an alternative gets us together. It makes us a movement that abolishes the present state, thinking and doing things differently. It refuses to adhere to any tidy definition, and that's okay. It goes against the grain, pushing against the naturalisation of social media, digital devices, impeded human needs, and modified behaviours in our lives. It incorporates critical thinking into our work. It brings back weirdness and fun.

DREAMING IN FORWARD MOTION

This is a vision for creative work that does more than churn out derivative 'content'. One that strives to do more than study so-called 'optimisations' that deliver invasive extraction to its creators and deep unhappiness to its receivers. We know full well that this is a sad application of artistic energies. We are fully aware that our physical and psychic selves are suffering.

Creativity is as estranged from itself as we are from each other.[‡7]

CINDY MILSTEIN

Here is a call to both creators and commissioners. Enough with the incessant digi-ideas. Move on from the reflexive use of social media as a solution.[§] When did you buy into this deprived lens of possibility? When did we collectively decide to dismiss anything beyond a screen as irrelevant, ridiculous, or impossible? If your answer is that budgets were reduced, that online experiences are more effective for 'engagement' and sales, that digital communication is more relevant today than IRL, or that offline options are always more expensive than online ones – the brainwash was successful.

Creativity-as-work loves to digitise everything under the assumption that 'offline' now represents the past. And it chooses to ignore the detrimental effects on mental health, social bonds, and creative and moral imaginations at large. Of course, it is a fantastic dream for the commissioners (as well as heads of agencies, design directors, mid-level managers… all levels of pseudo-powers) of creative labour to live in. In their vision, it is possible to sit behind a computer and magically 'reach' those delectable millennials, Gen-Zs, and (INSERT OTHER GENERATIONAL TAGS HERE) with 'content' that leaves a lasting impression on them – an impression that means they cannot forget nor resist whatever product or service is being offered. The job is done, the numbers achieved, and they never even had to leave the comfort of their desk chair.

THIS TECH-DETERMINISM PERSISTS FOR MULTIPLE REASONS. THE FIRST IS THAT IT IS BELIEVED TO BE MEASURABLE AND EFFECTIVE FOR ELUSIVE METRICS LIKE RETURN ON INVESTMENT (ROI). THE SECOND IS THAT IT IS EASIER AND CHEAPER TO MAKE (HIRING A PERSON TO MAKE SOME SOCIAL POSTS IS EASIER AND CHEAPER THAN ORGANIZING AN EVENT, ESPECIALLY IF THEY CAN BOTH DESIGN AND WRITE IT!). AND THE THIRD IS THAT IT MAKES SOME PEOPLE VERY RICH (FROM THE COMPANIES SELLING ONLINE ADVERTISING, TO THE BOSSES WHO NEED TO PROVE NUMBERS FOR THEIR BONUSES) WHICH MAKES IT BENEFICIAL TO PERPETUATE EFFICACY MYTHS. [§]

GET REAL

Do those commissioning our work not want to be well regarded? Organisations, institutions, and brands are all defined by the real-world connections they create. It is there that long-term bonds are built. Respect and advocacy come when someone feels their life has been affected positively – not subjected to a stream of posts, promotions, and mainstream marketing slush. This could be an event, an interaction, or an experience with something tangible (like a person, an activity, or a product). These interventions are most influential when they are delivered with a hands-off sensibility that speaks of generosity and thoughtfulness. For those wanting to stand out rather than fit in, offline expressions of creativity reign supreme. Can you think about the receiver more than you think about yourself?

The brands/people/initiatives we care about most are those less focused on promise and more focused on proof. It's easy to paint a (misleading) picture with your communications and make grand claims – what you believe in, what drives you, descriptions of how your audience will feel when they experience 'who you are' – but to prove it is much harder. It's about actions, not words. Less talk, more do. When journalists probed Miles Davis on his return from a rumour-ridden five-year disappearance from the public eye, clearly hungry for a sensational story, he cut them down for dramatising the absence. 'Okay, how would you say it then?' they responded. Davis stared down the barrel of the camera, picked up his trumpet without a word, and played.

TALK LESS

DO MORE

VALUE AND VALUES

This is where offline connections and happenings create a separation. A separation between the dull and the vibrant. The forgettable and the memorable. In the tunnel of 'digital-first' thinking, do you ever find yourself asking 'what is it that we're really *creating* here?' When there are numbers to be met, we eliminate what would be more imaginative, more enjoyable to make, and certainly more enjoyable to receive. Creativity as work compromises itself under this situation, where money and time are the quantitative economic terms that we measure everything against. Of course, we know this is flawed.

We can laugh deeply with a friend and know that the sensation cannot be replicated by anything money can buy.[§]

WE KNOW THE COST OF EVERYTHING
AND THE VALUE OF NOTHING

So when the current way of measuring what's valuable – this striving for ever greater growth and profit – is depleting us on all levels, not to mention the entire earth itself, is it that outrageous to think differently about value?

Such recognition is the first step toward valuing our world, toward knowing we can self-manage the whole of our lives... But it can only come when our artisanal efforts are part of crafting a social beauty.[§§]   CINDY MILSTEIN

In their book *Facing Value*, Maaike Lauwaert and Francien van Westrenen dive head-first into this problem, addressing the urgent need for alternatives. There are other ways of perceiving value, of deciding what is valuable, and of considering who can create value. The two argue that society could be driven by a different set of core values than 'maximization, growth for the sake of growth, and financial benefit.'[+8] They propose a radical reconfiguration, where the values driving how things are done and how people are treated are qualities such as care, trust, complexity, diversity, and humanity.
'...some will think these qualities are too soft and impossible to measure... But these (very often) old values are here among us, everyone knows when they are at work, they are felt and perceived. We believe they are as real as money, success, and meeting deadlines.'

'FRIENDSHIP IS THE FORCE THAT TRANSFORMS DESPAIR INTO JOY'   [§]
– FRANCO 'BIFO' BERARDI. YES!

IN OTHER WORDS, WHEN OUR ART AND CREATION WORK TOWARDS BEAUTY THAT IS   [§§]
NOT JUST AESTHETIC OR PROFITABLE, BUT ALSO SOCIALLY GLORIOUS. BUT ALSO
SOCIALLY GLORIOUS.

'Value' is immaterial, personal, and shifting. However, the plural *values* (care, compassion, reciprocity) are something we can agree upon. These offer a meeting point, a common ground that we find natural, despite their being more ephemeral. From the perspective of these reconsidered qualities, can we rethink value and construct a new vision? A reconsideration for offline action (and inaction) opens up new paths for what we value, what we want more of, and what we want to move away from. Can you imagine creating work that would not hinge on exploitation and manipulation? Could you envision a creativity that does not replicate the culture of distraction and destruction, and instead seeks to give more than it takes away?

Without constant awareness, we almost unwittingly take up the project of this society of control, with its fragmentation, insecurity, and shallow infotainment.[7]

CINDY MILSTEIN

Such 're-valuing' will fracture the core foundations of how we work, live, and assess life. It is obvious that we need an overhaul of how we think about value. And it is equally clear that our current measures of 'value', like some systematic vampire, are sucking away the *creativity* from our 'creative' jobs. What is the point of work that supposedly allows for creativity if not to be a place for new and experimental ways of thinking?

READ THIS:
IDEAS THAT MAKE NO MONEY HAVE NO MERIT.

DO YOU BELIEVE IT?

Where do we begin? Think forwards. Think value and values that look hard at what is already there, rather than trying to start again and making something new. What do we already have? The joys that are born when we socialise and get together IRL. These we know are paramount. Collective joy beats consumerist joy! The desire for a wake-up, for enlivenment and a different direction – that too is a force that's already there. A pleasure for altering what exists and the ability to envision what is yet to. Got it. A criticality and know-how to work against the grain. Check. The privilege and access (assignments, projects, contacts, and tools) to integrating form and content into the everyday. Sure, that's our job!

Rather than attempting an earthquake-sized change, imagine a seeping flood that inches in through our consistent input. Imagine integrating these new considerations – the recentring of offline approaches, the integration of thoughtful techniques, or even just conversations with others about this concept – into our simple everyday. In his essay titled *'A Liquid Revolution, for a Society Without Management, Money and Political Representation,'* writer and theatremaker Jan Ritsema speaks of revolution like a liquid; it starts small 'and then spreads like water, infiltrating, borderless, able to solidify as well as to evaporate.' Work with what you've got. Influence what you have access to. These deliberate decisions about what exists are where we can take off from.[§] No need to think up a brand new concept and struggle attempting to realise it. Instead: 'Think baby steps, think close.'[‡9] What are you doing today that could recentre what we value most? The definition of offline is a possibility space.

Futures are inscribed in the present
as imminent possibilities...[‡10]   FRANCO 'BIFO' BERARDI

'WE DO, WE WILL MAKE, WE WILL CREATE, WE WILL DEVELOP, WE WILL SHAPE, WE WILL   §
PROPOSE. WE WILL DO AS WE CANNOT NOT DO. WHO WANTS TO JOIN? WHO WANTS TO
SHARE WITH ME? SHALL WE BUILD A MOUNTAIN OF MONEY, OR OPEN A JOINT BANK
ACCOUNT?' - JAN RITSEMA

P029

ANTI–TREND   FORECASTS
Futurology   in   the   Creative   Industries

Trend forecasting has become a big business. It comes as no surprise. Futurology is nothing new, humans have always had an obsession with the future and desire to control it. Combine this with rapid technological developments, contemporary beliefs in furious economic growth, mantras of 'timing is everything', and thinking of creativity as a skeleton key, and you have a fertile environment for people hungry to be told what to do and how to do it. One leading trend forecasting agency claims to offer 'Proprietary Trend Intelligence: We give clients a glimpse of the future long before the rest of the world discovers it'. Try to contain your laughter. Do trend forecasters moonlight as horoscope writers too? These 'futures' are futures by decree. A future on rails. For the creative worker, purchased trend forecasts are brought to the table as a blueprint to be copied. Rather than a useful input, they have become an outsourcing of the creative part.

'THE FUTURE' IS A BUSINESS

From the beginning, trend forecasts are dubious in suggesting that some elite gathering has predictive abilities and others don't. Even beyond this, the business of selling 'what's next' is problematic. Here are some reasons why:

1.   These businesses frame cultural movements as tidy packages that can be sold. A product to be deconstructed and emulated in a different context.

2.   The majority of what forecasters sell is self-fulfilling. For example, fashion 'forecaster' WGSN has 50% market share. Customers buy their reports as insurance that the clothes they make will be in step with the market. Of course, this means at least half of all fast fashion retailers are being sold the same trend reports and produce their clothes accordingly. WGSN's 'predictions' are what generate trend cycles.

3. If you took the money spent on predictions and future speculation and instead used it to do something that responded to the current moment – something presently active – your project, brand, or organisation would be far more relevant.

Buy Now! The Youth Futures Report.
UNDER$TAND MILLENNIAL$! G€N Z!

Nobody can really predict or forecast trends. If forecasters can claim accuracy rates of up to 80%, it is because their predictions are self-driving. WGSN CO-FOUNDER MARK WORTH

Chasing future forecasts wastes time, energy, and resources that, if applied to the present moment, would have a far greater impact. When you create for the moment, you know you're responding to what is happening. When you create based on a forecaster's could-be, should-be, may-be predictions, you're taking a gamble on that. If things go afield, the forecaster doesn't care. They walk away, hands clean. There is zero accountability.

NOW NOT NEXT

Paying attention to what is happening in the present is the clearest read on where we are going and what is required. Noting historical factors is part of this awareness too. This 'skill' is ingrained in creative work and so naturally goes unnoticed. This is part of our practice; we don't need to name it. By paying attention to the nuances of now, we have a powerful ability to remain receptive to societal, cultural, and market-based change. You know, 'relevance'.

MAGIC AND DATA

We can all agree that the modern day prophet is a myth. Gifted fortune-tellers who sit calmly with closed eyes as future trends come to them do not exist. The contemporary alternative to this creative psychic is big ol' data. Data collection and AI are starting to compete with 'traditional' trend forecasting. Collating data from retailers' IT systems or using search data (Google has launched a 'trend spotting' division making reports based on this) is the latest way to bundle up so-called predictions into a product that can be sold. However, at the time of writing, the most recent study found that the best predictive models get it wrong more than half the time.[+1] The machines are programmed to identify and minimise emerging erratic behaviour, meanwhile the masses are growing more anxiously frantic by the day. They say data analysis is still in its infancy, though perhaps the rich arrays of human behaviours are too crazed to reduce to a set of percentages. No matter the reality, the rise of data extraction has driven the trend-forecasting business to become even more pedantic.[+2]

What desire feeds the notion that big data can be transformed into a knowable, manipulated, gamed, anticipated, pre-empted, capitalized and controlled life?[+3]

DATA PREVENTION MANIFESTO BY THE PLUMBING BIRDS

Let's take a moment to have some fun reading this excerpt from a popular forecaster's 'methodology' explanation:

Our Unique Methodology! We call it Cultural Triangulation, a three-pronged process of interrogation, observation, and strategic intuition that enables you to use a quantitative, qualitative, and expert-driven set of processes to analyse, interpret, and frame all decisions about future risk within a brand, consumer, and organisational context that is provable, practical, and minimises uncertainty.

Whoa.

Surveillance capitalism's economic imperatives were refined in the competition to sell certainty.[+4]

SHOSHANA ZUBOFF

Yes, humans have an annoying unpredictability about them that data sets would prefer to ignore. We're not that simple. In a conversation with the Editorial Director of trend forecasting agency *The Future Lab*, media theorist Douglas Rushkoff made a case for our complexity:

Part of this I would argue is your fault. Part of this is the futurists' fault. The beauty of the digital age was that we were going to create the future. The future became a topic. Not just a topic of conversation, but of creative potential. We saw the digital future, the digital Renaissance, as unbridled capacity of the collective human imagination to create any reality we wanted.

Then, when Wall Street came into the digital future they wanted to know stock futures, they wanted Futurists not to tell them what could be, but what will be. Because they want to bet on it. So then they're looking at 'how do we reduce uncertainty and create the most predictable outcome?' and it turns out the problem in the accuracy of a future forecast is these pesky humans and all their novelty and unpredictability.

So we create algorithms that have no purpose other than to reduce human novelty. To reduce that 20% of people who are not going to follow up with what the algorithm says – get that down to 10, get that down to five! Because human activity, human novel behaviour, that to the forecasters is noise. That's what it is called, 'noise'. And I'm arguing that the noise is the thing... That noise is what keeps us going.

Noise is where the new ideas come from.

Noise is where that weird liminal stuff that makes us human happens, so I want to bring up the noise! That's where human potential is.[‡5]

I go to live music to enjoy the mistakes.   V. VALE

EMBRACE THE NOISE

Invoke a schism in the serious. Blow off that ongoing *minimalism*. The dry Scandinavianisation of eeeeeeverything. Do us a favour and freak out a little bit today. Rushkoff told me: 'The one good thing about this whole phenomenon is that it gives people like us the ability to influence the future however we want'. He's right. Boring, homogenous 'trend' forecasts set the perfect stage for acts of deviation to stand out. Trend forecasts are just another consumer product for sale. Available to the masses, trend forecasts exploit our anxieties around being irrelevant or outmoded. This is a business driven by the fear of being unable to keep up. In buying trend forecasts, we buy into the same flat future sold to everyone else.

It is another case where blinders on is best. Avoiding exposure to bland, mass-market 'predictions' can help us protect original thought. Us pesky humans are good at imagination! We can make all the weirdness that data sets would prefer to eliminate. Algorithmic suggestions are just the continuance of restricted ideas. As music and tech writer NM Mashurov notes in an article for online magazine *Real Life*, 'The prevailing belief is still that computers are meant to eliminate human error, not perpetuate it.'[6] The world as it is happening around us right now is all we need to know. It is the perfect setting to cultivate new ideas. It is chock-full of the weird *liminal stuff* that makes life exciting – and that forecasts could never generate. Walk around with your eyes open and your headphones out.

Talk to people and engage with all the oddity that lies around you. Once distractions are removed we can hone in and see our senses deepen. This is how we connect the dots. The natural analyses. This is how previously unseen paths suddenly become visible. Focus on the now and the rest will follow.

Look up and look out. From your phone, from the floor, from the screen, out of the window and importantly out of yourself. There lies the power and inspiration.[7]

NADIA IDLE

MILLENNIAL   MELTDOWN

The	Everyday	Adoption
of	Marketing	Jargon

MILLENNIAL SUPERSTITION

Let's hazard a guess that one of the world's most overused words is 'millennial'.[§] It's not very exciting. But what else could we expect from a piece of marketing jargon that made its way into day-to-day speech?[§§] A word designed not to describe a band of people but a segment of consumers, and now used to stereotype a massive age-group. Hold your OK Boomer quip. It's all just ageism, normalised.[§§§] Adopted into our vernacular without critique. Who noticed? Who cares? We swim in a sea of marketing. It soaks into our everyday life, our leisure, our supermarket decisions, the media we read, stealthy inserted into the shows we watch. It's in the conversations we have, the techniques we use to construct our public images, our online personas.

[§] THE CONCEPT OF 'THE MILLENNIAL' HAS GIVEN ME GRIEF THROUGHOUT MOST MY CAREER. RECEIVING BRIEFS THAT SEEK TO CAPTURE THIS MYTHICAL CREATURE – APPEAL TO IT, ENGAGE WITH IT, BE LOVED BY IT. ALL DIRECTED BY THE RIDICULOUSLY-OUT-OF-TOUCH-WITH-REALITY BOSS OF COURSE. WE WENT TO ALL SORTS OF MAD LENGTHS, ANSWERING ALL SORTS OF IMPOSSIBLE REQUESTS, CENTRED AROUND A POPULAR STEREOTYPE. NOT TO MENTION, BEING REFERRED TO AS ONE WHEN IT SUITED. IT OFTEN FELT LIKE I HAD BUILT A CAREER BEING THE TOKEN MILLENNIAL AT THE TABLE.

ONE THING REMAINS TRUE, IF YOU WANT TO MAKE SOME EASY MONEY, START SELLING MILLENNIAL TREND-REPORTS.

[§§] DID YOU SEE THAT TRAGIC COCA COLA BILLBOARD INTRODUCING A NEW CAN THAT SAID '...BECAUSE YOU'RE AN EARLY ADOPTER'?

[§§§] EXEMPLIFIED BY ALMOST ANY GENERALISING ARTICLE AND THEIR ICY TITLE. FOR EXAMPLE, 'WHY MILLENNIALS ARE SO ENTITLED' – SWAP OUT 'MILLENNIAL' FOR THE WORD 'WOMEN' OR 'IMMIGRANTS', AND IT BECOMES A LOT LESS COMFORTABLE.

We are all marketeers, either by choice, by nature, or by necessity. Whether you're a freelancer or a full-time employee, the constant refashioning and reinventing of ourselves is (an exhausting) part of the job. Marketing the self tries to safeguard its future. The marketing of our very existence is now so normalised as to become invisible. It comes as no surprise, then, that such 'psychographics' are accepted as real reflections of the world, a useful way to categorise reality.[§] Such metrics instantly translate people born between two bookending years into a cute consumer profile. Quick. Snappy. Effortless.

THE 'M' WORD

'Millennial' is a generalist's dream. The dream to sweep a large age bracket into five crisp bullet-points. If this sweep defies logic, it still goes unchallenged in compacting a white, hetero, middle to upper class experience into a single category. In this it has been wildly successful, providing the perfect package to market – and to market to.

Particularly common is the use of 'millennial' as an excuse, explanation, or sales pitch. Millennial is the word that can be whatever you want it to be! Did somebody bail on their invitation to your party last minute? *eye roll* Millennial. Or do you need to convince a potential client of your agency's capabilities? 'Don't worry, we've got a team of Millennials right here!' Whether insult, argument, or justification – the M word can do it all.

Along with its flexibility, the M word can also be used to flex an organisation's incisive understanding of an entire generation. Drop the magical M for some pseudo-anthropological expertise, suggesting that one understands the mechanics and characteristics of this elusive social group.

'We know that millennials have the tendency to [INSERT DESIRED OUTCOME HERE].'

'[INSERT TRAIT OF CHOICE HERE] *is typical millennial behaviour.'*

'Most millennials will [INSERT PREFERRED BEHAVIOUR HERE].'

[§] DIFFERING FROM DEMOGRAPHICS, WHICH ARE FACTS SUCH AS GENDER, AGE AND INCOME, PSYCHOGRAPHICS 'SEGMENT A MARKET' USING 'DIMENSIONS' LIKE PERSONALITY TRAITS, INTERESTS, ATTITUDES AND GOALS, TO CREATE BUYER PERSONAS.

Let's get real, these ageisms are only the fulfilment of that human desire to categorise and understand the unpredictable. Not science. Not cultural insight.

AREN'T WE ALL MILLENNIALS?

Did you ever hear a description[§§] for the word 'millennial' and think 'that sounds like everyone'? Take *Financial Times* business columnist Pilita Clark's 'entitled, self-obsessed, job-hoppers, desperate for a life outside work, a "purpose", and constant feedback, except if it's remotely critical.'[‡1] Is this not a list that describes life in the contemporary West, a concise description of the bourgeois, regardless of your birthdate? Workers of all ages are far more alike than dissimilar when it comes to attitudes and values towards work. The notion that we should be finding meaning and a sense of purpose in our day jobs has integrated into society at large. It's not limited to a certain age group. Today, those aged 50+ are also concerned with their work/life balance, with having some job security, and with spending time on things that they're passionate about. Younger workers have moved jobs more than older people for decades, that's the time when it is safest to experiment. Reporter Akane Otani explains: 'The time to hustle is when you're young. Because unless you're a fantastic anomaly, you'll probably see your last big raise well before your 40th birthday.'[‡2] On top of that, the rise of the 'gig economy' and precarious labour has turned workers of all age groups into unwilling job-hoppers. As for the 'need for constant feedback', is that not the craving of anybody posting on social media? Millennial profiling, when it points the finger at 'youth today', echoes the way older generations have always judged the young – as spoilt, lazy, and frivolous.

Same script different day. We (millennials) are always the problem, never the solution.[‡3]   JULIANNE HARRIS

GOOD LUCK FINDING A STABLE AGE RANGE OR OVERALL EXPLANATION OF WHAT CON-
STITUTES AN ELUSIVE MILLENNIAL. IT TENDS TO DEPEND ON WHO IS USING IT AND
THE CONTEXT THE WORD IS BEING USED IN AS TO WHAT TRAITS WILL BE GIVEN OR
HIGHLIGHTED.

THE FUTR IS CRINGEY

London hosts the annual THE FUTR summit, an event formally known as 'Millennial 20/20'. Millennial 20/20 was formed specifically to discuss how to sell to millennials, until the conference's co-founder Rupa Ganatra opened its 2018 edition by saying that Millennial 20/20 was over. Ganatra explained it had become clear that retailers needed to understand a lot more 'than just the digitally savvy millennial generation.'[‡4] From now on, the conference would be rebranded to the cringey vowel-deprived FUTR. When questioned about the change, Ganatra explained there is now a 'millennial mindset' that has nothing to do with age. In other words, millennials do not exist. Some consumers may have grown up in a digital world, but the rest of society lives in it too.

SCREENS WITHOUT AGE

Perhaps the premier complaint about Millennials, Gen-Zs, or younger stereotypes is the amount of 'screen time' they consume. These 'digital natives'[§] are admonished for having the deepest dependencies on technology. On a good day, this may be reported as being 'savvy'. On a bad day, this group is simply 'addicted'.

I pondered. If 'youth today' are so screen-obsessed, how is it that my parents, uncles, aunts, and older colleagues and superiors are on theirs more than me? They bring their devices to the dinner table, cannot have days without email, keep their phones calmingly visible on the table at meetings, or fail to recognise the awkwardness of letting their attention be robbed by a notification during an active conversation. This observation is not wrong. It turns out older folk spend more time on their screens each day than the young – at least in America. The Economist reports that 'Americans aged 65 and over spend nearly ten hours a day consuming media on their televisions, computers, and smartphones. That is 12% more than Americans aged 35 to 49, and a third more than those aged 18 to 34 (the youngest cohort for whom market-research firm Nielsen has data)'.[‡5]

WHY THE OBSESSION WITH AGE?

We are in love with age tropes because we delight in packaging people up. Life's too complicated if each person is distinct, different from one another. It's comforting to think we are all the same, somehow. Without easy classification, marketing gets much harder. Consumers ought to be homogenous. Please let them be a uniform beige blob.

Targeting consumers based on age is a traditional tactic. It's what makes the concept of millennials (and all other age-based market segments) familiar. As digital data collection emerged, full-on age profiling blew up and has become the crux of online advertising, '... used by marketers so that they may be as efficient as possible with advertising products or services and identifying any possible gaps in their marketing strategy.'[6] Age profiles and their easy access are what digital marketers and online advertising agencies promise to their customers, and what the customers want to be true. The role of online platforms in proliferating and popularising the generated myth of Millennials also cannot be overlooked. No doubt it was to sell more media. Did you see how swiftly marketing budgets shifted there? Social media scared companies in that direction 'because it's where all the young people are! Reach them here. Target them now!' The millennial myth is a social media dream. You can hear the clicks from here.

THE ENDLESS ALLURE OF YOUTH

'Millennial' as a buzzword caught on fast and hard since youthfulness has undying appeal. Marketers have long lusted for a cool young customer over an ageing one. Society has historically been preoccupied with the younger end of the population. 'Western culture has always been obsessed with the foundational mythology of youthful energy. Not only sex, but also politics, arts, beauty, all worship the cult of energy.'[7] But as the young become increasingly jaded and poor, wouldn't the consumer who is older and wealthier be preferential?[§§] As advertising commentator Bob Hoffman puts it: 'Brands hate old people'. They have always chased younger customers, hence why they're so obsessed with the consumer personas of Millennials or Generation Z, even though we are currently experiencing the largest demographic change in human history. The world's population is ageing. Across the globe, the population segment aged 65 and over is growing faster than all other age groups.[8] Despite this surge, 'It is being completely ignored by the absurd marketing and advertising industries' continues Hoffman.[9]

'PEOPLE OVER 50 ARE RESPONSIBLE FOR OVER 50% OF CONSUMER SPENDING IN THE US. IF AMERICANS OVER 50 WERE THEIR OWN COUNTRY, THEY'D BE THE 3RD LARGEST ECONOMY IN THE WORLD – BIGGER THAN JAPAN, GERMANY OR INDIA.' – THE LONGEVITY ECONOMY, OXFORD ECONOMICS   §§

*...Age segmentation is lazy, and we can do better.
I am not saying that age is irrelevant. Of course it is
a factor... But age isn't enough to draw us together.*[10]

TANYA JOSEPH

TELL A LIE LONG ENOUGH,
AND YOU START TO BELIEVE IT

We easily accept the superstitions of birth-era categories resulting in common characteristics. With enough emphasis and repetition, we even begin to believe them. The idea that all of our behaviours and tendencies can be reduced to a birth year is highly appealing. When we read about our 'age profile', there is comfort in the idea that our experience of life is predetermined by our generation category, and that we have little control over it. Age category traits give us the excuse to live in a prescribed way. Through the lens of the category, we perceive our lives as having already been mapped, playing out with certain dynamics due to our circumstances.

MOVE ON FROM 'MILLENNIAL'

Enough with categorising each other into dull, incorrect ageisms. Don't find yourself unconsciously playing into the marketing jargon of our times. Police your mind, keeping it from creeping into your brain and speech without question. Quit promoting stereotypes like they're science. Be critical of the fiction that both surrounds and supports creative work. Let's go, it's time to move on from millennials.

FROM POSSESSION TO ACTIVITY
The Humanisation of Commercial Creativity

The full humanisation of man requires the breakthrough from the possession-centred to the activity-centred orientation, from selfishness and egotism to solidarity and altruism.[1]　　PHILOSOPHER, ERICH FROMM

Creative work needs a radical correction of course. A severe change of orientation. It is a shift from possession-centred to activity-centred. From cash-driven, to solidarity-driven. From obtrusion to a more conscientious mode of communication. From self-interest to altruism. Admitting you pay the rent by working in commercial creativity needn't be served with a side of cringe.

CONSCIENTIOUSNESS AND ALTRUISM

Conscientiousness and altruism: two principles we consider incompatible with capitalism and commercial work. Or are they? If we change what we seek, we can change the approach. Adopting an offline-first approach allows for quality of life and pleasure to become the new priorities and metrics of experience – possibilities that exist in a different space than the current internet's landscape. When the work is giving, what is received in return is equally enriched: qualities of trust, a reputation for the radical, an air of confidence, and a stark differentiation. These are the kind of qualities that are highly desired yet rarely achieved from the traditional tactics of marketing and branding. There are more ways to measure ROI. There is more to aim for than hard numbers and sales.

Somehow whenever I've worked with old-school creative directors or department leaders, they never get that when you're less pushy and understand the audience on the receiving end of a campaign, it is one million times more effective than shoving a brash sales message down a channel and putting some money behind its promotion. Connecting in real life has a sense of respectability and sophistication. It triggers something below the surface. It reverberates. It has effects that are powerfully invisible and delicately visible at the same time.

When we work with conscientiousness and altruism, we reach out with the intention to relate rather than control. It takes empathy and confidence. A confidence to go against norms. A confidence which most creative work (and its leaders) sorely lacks. We like to believe that everything we create is made with love and deep meaning. That our work stands out and goes beyond the status quo – but, does it? Sadly we often witness manipulation of 'consumers' rather than a consideration for fellow humans. We see fear more than we see care.

To act with altruism is to take an interest in improving the quality of life of whomever stands before your creation. In the context of creative agencies and answering client briefs, I've repeatedly witnessed how the action-reaction chain of offline actions that are conscientious and generous produce responses that boring social posts and sneaky e-com antics could never come close to. We once convinced a client to switch from using their billboards to advertise products and drive revenue, to rotating quirky visuals. The abstract colours, textures, words or illustrations were visually soothing, and sometimes tongue-in-cheek, emotionally lifting. No explanations. A tiny little logo (unavoidable to keep them happy). It was an attempt to de-advertise the landscape in favour of something kinder. Less aggressive and obtrusive. The client ended up being immensely proud of deviating from expectation. They received positive feedback from not only an external audience, but from their internal people. This had never happened before. This workplace had a notorious reputation for internal discontent. It was the first time employees saw their company stepping outside the norm and making such a kind gesture. They were impressed. Commendations flowed. It was the first time in years that the company had gotten any marked public attention.

CHILLING OUT

A common brief is 'we want to reach a new (read: younger) target audience'. More often than not, the commissioner then answers their own request with 'we need a social media strategy!' Yawn. Is that how far your imagination stretches when thinking how to connect with 'young people'? Somehow it persists that the only answer to any commercial challenge is a digital one.

One of my favourite examples illustrating the power of offline happenings is the result of a brief received from a jeans company to create a 'brand activation'[§] that would reach 'millennials and Gen-Zs of the creative class' (I can hear you dry retching, it's okay, I promise it gets better). The brand had a history of collaborations in the music industry, so we joined together with a radio station/record label in the target city to produce a series of concerts. All events were free to attend, but most importantly, they were deliberately not recorded. There would be no possibility to watch it online later. You needed to be there.

On top of this strictly offline approach, brand aggression was dialled way back. All communication went out through the radio station, the events were hosted at their venue, and the line-up was assembled according to their recommendations. All this meant that the commercial partner had to take a back seat and chill out. Easier said than done. 'How will the audience know that we are behind the concert? We need to have product in the space. Our logo has to be behind the band onstage, and we should stage models in the audience wearing the new collection', commanded the company's Brand Director. 'That's not necessary', we explained. 'The crowd will know who is behind it, trust us. People will get it. They will leave there having had a great night, the kernel of respect towards the brand involved will have been planted. Don't worry, they will know you were involved. No logos necessary'.

We all love when brands are hands-off in their approach. It takes a rare confidence to behave that way, which is why it leaves a strong impression. Discretion exudes a coolness. It achieves the perception you want better[§§] than aggressive, traditional approaches. But if this relaxed approach is the cure for overly anxious brands, for many it can be a hard pill to swallow. When online methods are offering you hard (falsified) numbers to prove results, hit targets, and confirm that you're seeing your money back, it is easy to remain conformist and try nothing that deviates.

The myths around online advertising's efficacy need to be dispelled as strongly as people believe that newspaper adverts are old-school and irrelevant. Guess what? Newspaper, TV, billboards, and radio adverts are more effective than online videos and promoted social posts.[‡2]

The logic is simple. When you create a happening, face-to-face, with motivations of generosity and consideration, it is exponentially

HERE WE FIND YET ANOTHER PRIME EXAMPLE ON OUR JARGON SAFARI OF A BUZZWORD   [§]
THAT PLAGUES WORKPLACES.

THAT YOU KNOW BETTER.   [§§]

more enjoyable than something through your phone. In turn, it reflects more positively on whoever gave that experience. Did anybody ever have an ad pop up over what they were trying to watch and think: 'Wow, I am so pleased that advert interrupted what I wanted to do. What a cool brand.'?

AN ERUPTION OF IN-REAL-LIFE

How else can conscientiousness and altruism manifest themselves? One way is by deciding to only put creative outputs in places that don't compromise the audience's psyche or privacy. Taking a stand and being thoughtful in not using platforms that prey on negative emotions and collect data. This effects the creative worker because we are frequently the creators. We are in those rooms, at those tables, or getting that brief. The levels of influence in our hands are underestimated. Parlay your thinking on how an altruistic brand would be envisioning how to enhance a commute rather than interrupt it.

These values equally live in communication that drops pushy ('the ultimate... enviable... you deserve...') and condescending, guilt-inducing ('must have... your perfect... don't be left behind') language. It breathes in brands that are over the hunger for SEO metrics and relentless quantification. It can be found in those who consciously choose to think beyond click stimulation.

This line of thinking creates spaces to be together. Those with resources (i.e. those with marketing and communication budgets) could provide occasions that build social cohesion, allow diverse groups to bump into each other, and fortify the existing places fading from our surroundings. Far from being outmoded, public places like domains, community halls, libraries, sports clubs, and local pools are more important than ever. They provide places for young and old, places to know each other better. From social cohesion to collective resilience, these 'outputs' are powerful and effective. But the value of such offline creative actions do require a new kind of accounting, a new set of metrics. How expansive is our economics? How deep is our concept of value?

We all know that appearing in a feed is totally forgettable. Less online congestion, more altruistic action. This is the new vision for creative work. Moving from a possession-centred to an activity-centred approach means getting face-to-face and making stuff *happen*. It means charging up your imagination and radically putting somebody else's benefits before your own.

PURPOSE SMURPOSE
On Appropriated Crusades

At universities, one of the marketing models taught is the 4 Ps of Marketing: Product, Price, Promotion, and Place. This is what they call the 'Marketing Mix', the combination of factors that can be controlled by a company and manipulated in their marketing. All sorts of 'experts' have tried to add a 5th P – People, Personalisation, Participation, Purpose. It is the latter one by far that endures the most emphasis and supposed importance. The pressure is on Purpose.

To start your business based on a purpose is not unlikely. Examples are *this is Sweden*, an anti-racism fashion platform that decided to start using garments to address the topics of immigration, nationality, and Swedishness after seeing the far right gain political ground throughout their country. Born in Colombia, founders and fashion designers Pablo and Ana Londoño watched their adoptive country shift further right, causing them to ask: 'What can we do? We are not politicians, journalists, lawyers or policy-makers. What we have is creativity and a kin of activists around us.' Thus, *this is Sweden* was born. Another larger scale example is *Patagonia*. *Patagonia* began in the early 70s, making tools for outdoor climbers. Since then they have expanded their product offering, seeking to produce top-form outdoor gear that is environmentally and ecologically sensitive. Through the decades, their drive has remained the same: 'Build the best product, cause no unnecessary harm, use business to inspire and implement solutions to the environmental crisis.'[*1]

Both *this is Sweden* and *Patagonia* demonstrate admirable and important pursuits. They are two businesses born from a clear reason to exist in this world. Troubles arise when a purpose is shoe-horned in later, once a company or brand realises that to stand for 'something greater' may be lucrative.

In the trials of feeling something deeper from our day jobs, creative work can find us regularly asking 'what's the purpose?' It's our human tendency to seek inherent value. We want those *values* that run deeper than strong quarterly returns or satisfying graphic design.

Unable to find human value in the Art of Making People Buy Stuff, marketers invent a supposed deeper meaning to what they do. Their brands are not mere mortal manufacturers of goods and services, oh no. They are purpose-led knights on a crusade to change the world for the better. Sadly, this conveniently ignores that, well, they aren't.[‡2]

JP HANSON

LOOKING GOOD BY DOING GOOD

Companies will add an element of 'doing good' to their branding (not necessarily their business) in reaction to a perceived growing expectation for it. People expect businesses and brands to be conscious of their impact – socially, environmentally, ethically. Or do they? There is no doubt we increasingly hold them accountable for their actions, but how many of us expect any sizeable acts of selflessness from these businesses? The distinction between taking responsibility and a new marketing angle is often deliberately obscured. But we are not stupid. We can spot an attempt to 'look good' by doing good. In a piece for the *New York Times*, Erin Griffith addresses how baffling it is that these strategies continue:

And yet years after the HBO satire 'Silicon Valley' made the vacuous mission statement 'making the world a better place' a recurring punch line, many companies still cheerlead the virtues of work with high-minded messaging. For example, Spotify, a company that lets you listen to music, says that its mission is 'to unlock the potential of human creativity.' Dropbox, which lets you upload files and stuff, says its purpose is 'to unleash the world's creative energy by designing a more enlightened way of working.'[‡3]

The mistake is seeing Purpose as some sweet new branding element. 'Whatever you want to call it – greenwashing, whywashing, wokewashing – attempts to gain profit from social causes without investing in the time and resources needed to address the issues in meaningful ways are never well received.'[‡4] True purpose is intrinsic and natural. It conveys its importance openly and is visible without external communication. It is made clear through action and simple embodiment – no loud 'look-at-me' promotion necessary. In his take on 'brand purpose for the sake of brand purpose', author and marketing strategist JP Hanson highlights the rare nobility that can come from purposelessness:

Not every company must be purpose-driven – and there is nothing wrong with that. It is not meaningless work to market a brand that 'merely' pays its taxes and treats its stakeholders well. To claim otherwise would be absurd. Particularly given how few supposedly purpose-driven companies do.[‡5]

We can all recognise a purpose-ploy when we see one. Do they really think we are that gullible? A newly tacked-on purpose is as transparent as it is easy to spot. Old school ad-man Bill Bernbach cut to the essence of purpose when he said that 'a principle isn't a principle until it costs you something.' Today we could summarise the strategy as the opposite – 'it isn't a principle until it's making you money.'

WHEN PURPOSE BECOMES PITY

Purpose as a marketing strategy evokes sadness. We pity its attempt to matter. The executions are rarely poignant, since trying to connect on an individual level over a cause has such wide-ranging variation. How to catch the max amount of potential buyers with a single brand purpose? Go for something broad. Hit the lowest common denominator. Create vague communications that tout your 'sustainability', 'female empowerment', or 'pride'. Here we have another example of *when you say everything, you say nothing*. In effect, empty opportunistic bids for purpose don't differentiate. Rather than being voices for good, the guilty become echoes of one another. From a positioning perspective, brand purpose becomes pointless.[‡6]

The jury is out on the financial benefits of taking on a 'purpose'. Depending on whether you want to prove its growth-driving potential or its repulsion factor, there is 'data' to support you either way. From a creativity perspective, there are an infinite number of more transgressive ways to differentiate and get attention than adding on a shiny new passion as though it was there all along. Sudden 'dedications' read as the money-hungry afterthoughts that they really are. Repulsive and embarrassing rather than compelling. Why not skip the fake concern in favour of some real conscientiousness? If you want to shape public perception, get back to that key principle of less talk, more do. 'Actions speak louder...' Creating work that demonstrates care shifts away from dependency on mere digital communication to allowing real-life shake-ups. Easy noncommittal 'purpose' talk is cheap – and online communication has made it cheaper than ever. How to be different? Behave like it. Show it. No empty blabs – actions with altruism are identifiably different. No 'instaPurpose' necessary.

INTERLUDE
INTERLUDE
INTERLUDE
INTERLUDE
INTERLUDE
INTERLUDE
INTERLUDE
INTERLUDE

I

1. WHAT ARE YOUR HOBBIES?
     If it takes you longer than 10 seconds to come up with an answer,
     that's too long. Reclaim your free time.

2. IS IT JUST ME OR…
     do simply the words 'social media strategy' feel old?

3. BRAIN FOG IS BURNOUT
     When you sit down to a task and cannot separate your mind from
     scrambled eggs, that is a sign something needs to change.

4. SEARCH AND DESTROY
     A creativity that does not adhere to the mass celebration of mediocrity.
     That rebels against unremarkable minimalist hellscapes rather than
     appealing to them. This is what we're looking for. Are you missing
     a hobby?

5. WHY PR IS MADNESS
     If you know 'influencers' buy followers, why rank their 'influence' by
     follower count?

6. BRANDING DESPERATION
     A sure sign of a deflating situation is a new approach every half year.
     Swapping from platform to platform, tagline to tagline, 'purpose' to
     'purpose'. No consistency in a flurry of fail.

I

7. LIFE IS AN OFFLINE PLATFORM

Some of my favourite offline platforms include life, the unforeseen delight of a message written on a wall (including bathroom messages), book exchanges on the street, the sound of wind outside the window, abandoned grocery lists, hidden notes on bar coasters, real-life conversations, clothing, and faces.

8. EVERYTHING IS BRANDED. ANYTHING IS BRAND-ABLE

Schools, museums, city districts, universities, even whole countries! Branding has migrated out of 'traditional' commercial capacities to enter every area of what surrounds us. This reflects the mindset killing us quickly, that monetary value can be applied to anything and everything. That is why we promote doing and making 'Just Because', because no reason is a reason. Let's call it Post-Needing-A-Point.

9. ARE YOU BEHIND A CARROT?

Has your employer been dangling a promise in front of you? The promise of a raise? Better projects? Shorter hours? A stable contract? New challenges or responsibilities? These are dangled carrots and carrots are an exploitation tool that taps into hopes and aspirations, stringing us along with empty promises. Beware of work-for-hope being disguised as what it means to have a 'creative' career. Having a 'creative' occupation doesn't mean trading off sane, reasonable, and fair expectations of an employer.

Carrots are masking the collapse

of the cultural sector.

THE CARROTWORKERS' COLLECTIVE

I

10. STEAL BACK WHAT'S BEING STOLEN FROM YOU
Time. Dignity. Respect. If it isn't deserved, let's not give it.

11. THE PORTFOLIO SELF IS NO FUN
Maintaining a consistent image of your self and work can be murderous to the spirit. We are multifaceted and ever-changing. To portfolio the self flattens that complexity like a compressed accordion. Keep them on their toes. Fluctuate and deviate, fake it and be whatever you want to be that day. When the internet documents everything you do, we need to get creative with our bluffing. Bluffing for work = 100% shameless.

12. 'DOES SOCIAL MEDIA REALLY MODIFY BEHAVIOUR?'
'Did you always take your phone to the toilet?'

13. DISCOMFORT IS A CHANGE-CATALYST
To hope is to give yourself to the future – and that commitment to the future is what makes the present inhabitable.[‡1]
REBECCA SOLNIT

INTERLUDE

WE'RE IN TOTE HELL
The Proliferation of the Tote Bag

Boy, do I wish I had a dollar for every time I have been given or offered a tote bag. At events, in stores, even with online orders – the level of tote-dom has reached critical mass. Are we meant to find this 'sustainable'? The even wilder part is when one is meant to see this as a gift rather than a practicality. When you're leaving an event they give you an empty bag (!?). Let's not mistake this for an act of generosity. There is little altruistic motivation here. This is classic advertising. This is being not-asked to do work for free. Are we consciously and consensually working for that logo, or is it unpaid promotion? For many, the abhorrence at being not-asked to do unpaid work is immediate and visceral, while for others it can go unnoticed.

I'M YOUR NOT FREE BILLBOARD

ENTER THE STATUS TOTE

The Status Tote[§] is an emblem (and symptom) of current culture. The Status Tote sees the user deliberately carrying a certain branded tote not just as a hold-all but as a signifier about themselves. The logo on the bag is meant to tell others something about the person carrying it, something they are choosing to project. From museum totes and fashion brand totes, to event totes, band merch totes, even foreign-country-grocery-store totes...

...There's no denying that prestige tote bags are on the rise. Totes communicate in a more nuanced language now... A Judd Foundation option does a fine job of informing strangers you've been to Marfa, but a bag from the Get Go family-run supermarket there demonstrates a more discerning awareness of the local culture.[‡1]

Turns out there are also levels of in-the-know in the choice of tote too. There are shades of meaning, tints of nuance. Who knew the decision about a bag – and how you want the world to read you – could get so complex?

BACK TO VISUAL APPEAL

Even if you would like to produce totes, they have a higher likelihood of going cult if you do something beyond your logo on it.[§§] The visual identities of brands/projects/initiatives have never been more extensive. There is variation in quality, but good ones are easy to find and easy to make. It is no longer enough to simply whip up a logo, a typeface and a palette – et voilà. We have created entire visual ecosystems around brand identities. Responsive logos, counterpart-symbols and motifs, themes for imagery, hierarchies of typefaces, patterns and textures (are you more geometric or a playful doodle?), nuanced colour palettes and styles of animation, statements and aphorisms, compositional character and interaction movement... the list goes on.

Why is it then that there is such insistence on putting logos everywhere? Why develop such sophisticated identities if you're only going to use them in the most basic manner? Did you make that whole visual identity for it to sit in a 'deck'?

LOGO   OVERLOAD   =   BASIC

LOGO LAZINESS

Logo totes reek of that bad habit in commercial creativity where reflexive logo application happens in response to the comment 'it needs branding'. It is lazy creative that uses the logo as a design element. Creative-creative goes beyond the logo into the visual ecosystem and brings the project to life.[§§§] And, top-notch-creative-creative will make the output equally branded (read: recognisable) as sticking a logo on it – but in a manner exponentially more clued up, and visibly so. If your free tote bag had an illustration or a statement on it in your handwriting, your vibe, your palette, your typeface, your whatever, your everything – I may be more likely to consider it a gift. It certainly would be more likely to get used.

The Era of the Tote has reigned proud and strong. Here's hoping the end may soon be in sight. Unfortunately, I doubt it. But, perhaps you'll have a hand in that.

SAY THAT FAST AND IT SOUNDS EERILY LIKE STATUS QUO.   §

IT IS EASIER TO MAKE A CULT-TOTE THAN A CULT-BRAND.   §§

THIS IS WHAT WE CALL GOING POST-LOGO.   §§§

THE CULT OF DIGITAL
An Industry Brainwashed

The Cult of Digital (CoD) dominates today's sites of creative work. It is cult-like because of its mass of worshippers and invulnerability to fact. Nothing is more representative of our collective digital devotion than our smartphones. These are the devotional objects of the Digital. They function like a rosary, they are handheld, and they are readily available.[‡1] The delusions around digital-solutionism reign so strong, to question them is to call into question your own commitment to a project's success. The choices are stark: adhere to 'digital-first' or divorce from it at your own risk. The belief stands so unwavering, it is prioritised and naturally assumed to be the best possible route. Suggest otherwise and you could be labelled an offline romantic, out of touch with the world and more importantly, the *future*. By now you've noticed that there is zero conversation about possible alternatives. So why not keep quiet and follow suit? Don't be contentious now. Obey the movement and submit. After all, what's not to love? I mean besides imposing dullness with its limitations and greedily monetising our creativity... or besides the social and individual impacts of online-oriented lives... or besides the clear complicity with privacy-impinging and generally exploitative practices.

Digital advertising is not nice. There, we said it. Though, like anything popular, people will continue to believe it must 'work' due to its ubiquity. 'Surely it must be effective, otherwise why would everyone be doing it?', they argue. Yet, ask virtually anyone on the inside of the cultural industries exactly why or how online advertising works and you will struggle to find someone who can give a clear answer. Naturally, measuring efficacy depends on the objective – what do you want to get out of it, and how well can the chosen route achieve that? The measuring sticks on offer tend to be as arbitrary as the medium, from 'engagement' to 'return on investment (ROI)' and 'earnt reach'. These terms are a coded glossary for an industry that prefers jargon to truth.

Once we start questioning the CoD, we soon find ourselves in a dark, disorienting world. We're stuck in a confusing labyrinth, where even the walls are false. Here we will take a look at several of the delusions that persist and bring to light the complexity of the situation.

COMMON MISBELIEF

There is a long and unspoken history of social media advertising providing zero proof of its efficacy. In 2017, Marc Pritchard, brand head of the world's largest advertiser Procter & Gamble, gave a watershed speech that shocked the insular advertising world. Pritchard revealed that P&G had cut its digital advertising spend by USD\$200m and had seen no resulting impact on sales. In other words, they discovered what they were paying for had done nothing. Pritchard has subsequently become an open challenger of the effectiveness of digital marketing, and a proponent for cleaning up its 'murky' supply chain. Since then, more information has emerged from the shadows about how (in)effective online advertising really is. But it is far from public knowledge. For a moment there, it felt like the potential beginning of a wake-up. Alas, no. Digital ad spend, despite being unproven, continues to ramp up regardless. At the 2019 conference held by marketing trade organisation ANA, Pritchard stated:

Digital media continues to grow exponentially, and with it, a dark side persists, and in some cases, has gotten worse... Waste continues to exist from lack of transparency and fraud. Seven out of 10 consumers say ads are annoying, and ad blocking is accelerating. Privacy breaches and consumer data misuse keep occurring. Unacceptable content continues to be available and is still being viewed alongside our brands...[‡2]

Most creative directors[§] in hip agencies will still be pushing for social campaigns and 'digital takeovers',[§§] which all require financial injections in order to be seen or make it up SEO ranks – except now we know that advertising platforms can easily promise this, without any way to hold them accountable.

WHO IS LEADING THE DIRECTION WHEN THE DIRECTORS ARE ILL-DIRECTED? [§]

SOCIAL & FRAGILE: [§§]
THE CULTURAL INDUSTRIES ARE SUCKERS FOR 'DIGITAL TRENDS'. IF THERE IS A NEW PLATFORM, THEY'LL HESITATE UNTIL IT'S HAPPENING, THEN ARRIVE AT THE PARTY TOO LATE. PLATFORM POPULARITY CAN BE FICKLE, REVEALING THAT AN ELEMENT OF FRAGILITY EXISTS. REMEMBER WHEN SNAPCHAT WAS THE PLACE TO BE. 'ALL THE YOUNG PEOPLE ARE THERE'. VINE, TIK TOK, A NEW YEAR A NEW VERSION. THE FRA-GILITY WENT ON DISPLAY WHEN KYLIE JENNER TWEETED 'SOOO DOES ANYONE ELSE NOT OPEN SNAPCHAT ANYMORE? OR IS IT JUST ME... UGH THIS IS SO SAD'... AND SNAPCHAT LOSES USD\$1.3 BILLION MARKET VALUE OVERNIGHT. BOOM.

FICTION & FRAUD

When a company wants to advertise online, this could be putting money behind an Instagram post, or buying Google ads,[§] the seller of that advertising will offer them a deal that promises a certain ROI. These metrics may consist of how many people will see it or how many people will click the link.[§§] This process is undermined by the little-known crime of ad fraud. Ad fraud is that these supposedly guaranteed interactions are dominated by bots rather than real people. '...about 52% of traffic on the web is now human. The rest are bots and scrapers and hackers. Not all bots are marvelling. Not all bots are bad. Some of them have a purpose. But the number of fraudulent bots is staggering. It is believed now that at least $12 billion a year are being stolen by online criminals who are creating fraudulent clicks, fraudulent traffic, and fraudulent websites.'[+3] Imagine that, almost half of the traffic online is fictional! The world of the Cult of Digital sure is fantastical. Like a hallucination of reality, a vague tracing of its supposed resemblance. 'Digital is becoming the marketing industry's version of fake news. Digital is to advertising as Avril Lavigne is to punk rock.'[+4]

Essentially, what this means is that the majority of digital advertising paid to be seen by a live human being goes unseen. P&G's CFO Jon Moeller added to comments on their moment of revelation that they were in no rush to put money back into digital media, nor to see that advertising show up next to objectionable content.[§§§] 'Clearly we don't need to be spending money on content that is seen by a bot and not a person. Clearly we don't need to be spending money on ads that are placed in inappropriate places.'[+5] Those selling it don't care, they just want the money. Resources are wasted by the desire for numbers to prove budget spends and returns. It begs the obvious question: are digital delusions at the point where any number will do, no matter how knowingly false? Do we care so little about lies that we're willing to continue

[§] GOOGLE AND FACEBOOK DOMINATE THE ONLINE ADVERTISING SCENE. THE SITUATION IS COMMONLY REFERRED TO AS THE 'DIGITAL DUOPOLY'.

[§§] DID YOU KNOW, WHEN YOU CLICK THROUGH TO A WEBSITE (FOR EXAMPLE, THE NEW YORK TIMES) THERE IS AN INSTANT ALGORITHMIC AUCTION FOR THE RIGHT TO SHOW YOU AN ADVERT? IN THAT FRACTION OF A SECOND, ALL YOUR COOKIES HAVE BEEN PASSED ON BY NYT TO AN AD-SUPPLIER TO SHOW YOUR PROFILE TO THE BIDDERS, AND DETERMINE WHO WANTS TO BE DISPLAYED IN FRONT OF YOU THE MOST. 'ALL COOKIES ARE MADE PUBLIC IN THIS FASHION. I THINK PEOPLE DON'T REALISE THIS IS PART OF THEIR EVERYDAY INTERNET EXPERIENCE.'[+11] – SHENGWU LI

[§§§] FOR EXAMPLE, BUYING A YOUTUBE AD AND HAVING IT SHOW UP NEXT TO EXTREMIST CONTENT OR SOMETHING YOU CONSIDER UNSAVOURY.

giving away money because it's easier than confronting the truth? The truth being, nobody has the surefire way to get what you want – the ultimate prize – going 'viral'.

I have a secret love for the words 'going viral'. They take me back to days working for the aforementioned denim fashion brand. Two words that will forever bring a smile to my face after years in an environment where any video content was called 'making a viral'. The words video and viral became interchangeable. We never went viral. There was not the money nor the know-how to make an average production receive worldwide attention. The company's owner liked playing Creative Director. He had a cute naivety that thought organic reach was a thing and invisibly pulled PR strings were not. When his intimidating presence expected a viral video to be made – using mediocre 'behind-the-scenes' footage, filmed on the set of the campaign shoot, clearly directing the models to 'act casual and off duty' and turned black and white for a backstage look – the team found themselves in an impossible situation. This is what happens under the Cult of Digital. Misguided beliefs suggest anything is possible in the world of the internet. In reality the internet doesn't care about your crappy campaign video. Yawn. Skip. Forget.

JUST LIKE OVERWORK

Over-investment in digital is a definable characteristic of today's cultural industries. To become a meme is priceless. Pray for infamy. The price tag is just as slippery. Contemporary consumerist culture believes in branding, the brand as personality, the brand as essential for sales. 'Brand building' is the dominant request, whether using those exact words or something similar. Yet when it comes to the construction of the brand castle, online advertising fails to measure up.[§§§§] To advertise with the goal of brand building means that the advertising medium's most important attribute is visibility[§§§§§] and targetability. We have established how the majority of what is bought goes unseen. Targetability is the ability to target the right people in the right place at the right time.

[§§§§] OFFLINE ACTIONS EXCEL AT BRAND BUILDING AS THEY CREATE DEMAND (EXPOSURE TO SOMETHING NEW AND EXCITING) AND CAN FIT HAND IN HAND WITH ONLINE SUPPLEMENTS, WHICH CAN FULFIL IT (EASY ONLINE SHOPPING, STRONG SEARCH-ABILITY, ONGOING CONTACT AND INFORMATION). THE CLASSIC RECOMMENDED SPENDING-SPLIT IS 60/40 BETWEEN BRAND BUILDING AND SALES ACTIVATION, WITH NEW STUDIES SUGGESTING THE MAJORITY OF THAT BUDGET SHOULD BE PUT INTO 'TRADITIONAL' MEDIA SUCH AS TV, RADIO, OUTDOOR AND NEWSPAPERS.

[§§§§§] SEE 'WHAT'S HOT AND WHAT'S NOT' ON P062 FOR MORE ON VISIBILITY AND RELEVANCE.

When asked to rank which advertising mediums are the most effective and targetable, advertisers and agencies massively overrate the value of online video and paid social. The top six mediums for targetability are the traditional ones persistently proclaimed as 'dead'. Not only are 'traditional media' such as TV and radio the most effectively targetable, they also rank highest in ROI.[‡6] 'There is a clear disconnect between the scale of investment in online media and the value it delivers.'[‡7]

Research into the performance of certain marketing mediums consistently reveals that those dealing in digital marketing work have no clue. Digital marketing and media expert Paul Dughi is baffled by the lack of knowledge at the intersection of marketing and the digital. 'What's incongruous to me is that most marketers still don't know if it works. Seriously. Almost half of all of the marketers (surveyed) say they have *no ability to show the impact on their business.*[‡8] The truths of these bought communications are far from understood, let alone acknowledged. The Cult of Digital is under deep hypnosis, refusing to wake up and confront its own efficacy. Budgets continue to devote the lion's share to 'digital' and ideas for in-real-life happenings are considered irrelevant or 'too expensive'.[§] When creative work commits to the Cult of Digital, you worship with the rest of the congregation, or you're out.[§§]

A PEEK INTO THE BLACK BOX

The systems of online advertising in operation today have evolved out of adaptation rather than a deliberate initial vision. To deem them original inventions of evil genius gives them too much credit. Their bizarre set-ups and inability to explain their own devices is closer to fluke than masterplan. As ex-Silicon Valley tech worker Anna Weiner revealed: 'It's much more chaotic behind the screen. These organizations are messy, the products are messy, the code is messy, it's a lot less coherent than you might think.'[‡9]

In an interview with *Logic* magazine, behavioural economist Shengwu Li paints a remarkable picture of online advertising's absurdity, explaining the relationship between advertising platforms Google and Facebook, and those buying advertising from them (referred to as 'advertisers'). Li clarifies how Google developed an auction system for

[§] OVERLOOKED ARE THE INVISIBLE COSTS OF THE 'CHEAPNESS' OF DIGITAL MARKETING. PLATFORMS SUCH AS FIVERR, WHERE ADVERTISERS CAN GO TO GET QUICK, INEXPENSIVE CREATIVE WORK, ARE POPULATED WITH PRECARIOUS WEB DESIGNERS AND CONTENT COPYWRITERS. THESE ARE THE VICTIMS OF THE EXPLOITATIVE, POORLY ACCOUNTED FOR PRICING OF A QUICK, COST-CUTTING CAMPAIGN.

[§§] PROVERBIALLY IF NOT PHYSICALLY.

their sales model, which has advertisers bid on the different ad slots available. For example, how much are you willing to pay to be the top search result? And how much would you comparatively pay to be third? This is based on the key words searched and uses a method called the 'second-price auction'. The second-price auction sees everybody bid, then the highest bidder wins. That winner then pays the amount placed as the second-highest bid. Get it? So where the traditional ascending auction sees bidders decide dynamically when they want to quit, the second-price auction system means bidders decide upfront how much they value the object, and the auctioneer can ask everybody in advance for their bid instead of running the live ascending auction. What advertisers are bidding on is not the slot but the price per click – how much they are willing to pay Google every time their slot in the search results gets clicked.

How Facebook sells advertising is different. Rather than placing ads around search terms, Facebook says they will provide an advertising product that promises a personalised effect using the data they have – a person's gender, age, interests, online history, as well as more sensitive racial, ethnic, religious, and partisan attributes.[‡10] They use the information they have on their users and turn it into an offer to advertisers on how to calibrate their campaign. So rather than placing a bid, you tell Facebook what kind of ad campaign you want to run, and they go off to place bids on your behalf.

...That's the oddness of it. It's as if you went to a supermarket and rather than the owner saying, 'Here are all the prices, please buy what you want,' the owner says, 'Why don't you tell me how you're feeling this week and what you have a taste for, and I'll find the optimal bundle and tell you how much it costs. Don't worry, I know my warehouse much better than you do...' Facebook is saying, 'Tell us about your advertising campaign, and we will figure out what you would have rationally done if you had access to our troves of information.' Do advertisers not care about that lack of transparency?[‡11]

Li highlights that the 'black-box' element to Facebook's algorithm system means that its system runs on trust. 'When Facebook says they know better than you what kind of advertising you want to be buying, you really have to believe that Facebook has your interests at heart.'[§§§] It's a question that can hardly be said with a serious face. Would you trust Facebook? That smirk soon retracts when the answer is well... yes, we are. Using these platforms places unfathomable amounts of information into their hands. We just cross our fingers and hope everything will be alright. They are amassing this data, tidying it up into packages, and selling it on, all with our acceptance. They refuse to let us see exactly what it is they have and are actively collecting about us. And we comply.

Facebook shuts down tools developed to let the public see how users are being targeted by advertisers.[12] Browse the internet for guidance about healthy alcohol consumption, and on your next login you will quite likely find ads for discount alcohol appear.[13] Surveillance? Who cares. Never mind the facial recognition software. Cultivating discrimination, hate, and misinformation while feigning to be bastions of free speech who build positive communities?[14] It's fine.

Except it's not. There is no denying these mechanics are way past twisted. However, so accepting are we of data collection and this billion-dollar industry of platforms running in outrageous modes that we seem to have misplaced our outrage.[§] When did we lose our 'resistance-needed' alert? The radar got thrown out with the other analogue junk. Not only are we unalarmed by this digital control society, it's become normalised to the point where private information is no longer just for corporations. Now people have become interested in using it to target each other. The information advertisers have access to is so personalised that there are auctions where you can bid for an individual human impression. Thanks to some 'innovative' new startups, you can now run an ad campaign targeting a single person.

Maybe you want your partner to stop smoking. This startup will generate a special link for you that looks like it's an e-commerce site. You send it to your partner and when they click it, they get a cookie secretly loaded into their browser. This cookie enables the company to track your partner across the web. You write up an anti-smoking ad, and the company will ensure that your partner sees that ad everywhere. Now your partner's entire internet experience is permeated with pressures to stop smoking.

You can design a similar campaign for a coworker you don't like. You can show them ads for job-hunting websites, to encourage them to get another job.[15]

Whoa. How warped have we become? Willingly giving up our private data like it has no worth to us, contemplating methods to get workmates out the door, then accepting the word of these platforms. We trust their good intentions, even though the reality is precisely the opposite. Our morals went out with the tide, the pull of the Cult has

§ 'AIRBNB HAS A PATENT FOR AI THAT CRAWLS AND SCRAPES EVERYTHING IT CAN FIND ON YOU, THEN JUDGES WHETHER YOU ARE CONSCIENTIOUS & OPEN OR SHOW SIGNS OF "NEUROTICISM, INVOLVEMENT IN CRIMES, NARCISSISM, MACHIAVELLIANISM, OR PSYCHOPATHY." GOOD LUCK CHALLENGING THESE JUDGMENTS, TOO!'
- @FRANKPASQUALE TWEET ON 19TH JANUARY 2020.

them now. Madness and calamity mark the qualities of the situation we find ourselves in. The world of online advertising is absent of anything denoting quality. 'Creative'? Only the manipulation.

IN THE BEST INTEREST OF WHOM?

With lies, fantasy, fraud, and disinformation rife; it's clear how and why the Cult of Digital has no shortage of disciples. And if your job relies on this myth, why would you dispel it? So many roles in creative agencies exist due to the belief in digital efficacy. From digital strategists and designers, to digital directors, UX specialists and optimisation experts. As author Upton Sinclair once said: 'It is difficult to get a man to understand something when his salary depends upon his not understanding it.' Even today's graphic designers find themselves forced into digital art direction. They're more likely to be on assignment for online content than 'traditional' print material.

When online advertising is this dark ecosystem which performs far differently than what we perceive, what's so mesmerising? The dedication to a current going nowhere, doing nothing, for what?

I despise that creative work means making online advertising. I'm frightened that our work is complicit in this system. I'm confused that there is such complacency around the invasive and dishonest actions of these platforms. I don't understand the silence. Where is the opposition? There is more irritation at a slow loading page than distress that such exploitation is now part of the job. Is the ability to app-chat to each other and scroll through an infinite stream of photos really worth it? There are other places to kill time and other sites to read the news. There are options and alternative platforms that replicate these services precisely, and yet we sit here. Inert. Just like the distraction hypnosis, we are not moving. The Cult of Digital persists, unwavering.

Once we've laid it out like this, 'digital-first' starts to sound crazy. Considering something else seems like a saner option. Like those escaped from a cult, we look back in horror to how blind we were. Once the invisible is made visible, we cannot unsee it. The pages here represent only a speck of what's going on. Half a speck. Now you understand why alternatives to online-everything deserve consideration. Not as a meek voice of mere preference. Not as a quiet whisper trying to gather attention to non-digital solutions. But as a loudspeaker that blasts through the devotion. The Cult of Digital is a perversion in need of radical disclosure. Who is prepared to unsubscribe?

WHAT'S HOT AND WHAT'S NOT
Why 'Relevance' Lives Offline

Advertising is all about influencing our decisions and it used to be believed that this happened by subconsciously guiding our behaviour. The thought was that if an advert affected us emotionally, it planted a seed which could materialise later at a point of purchase. This may have once worked – though there are doubts since we are more rational and more difficult to influence than we give ourselves credit for. But today the mechanics of *relevance* are different when much of creative work is brand building rather than simply selling.

Relevance is as much a priority to sneaker brands as it is to modern art museums or art schools. Nobody wants to be irrelevant. To be relevant is to be on the radar. It is to be respected. In his 2017 series *State of the Culture*, Artnet critic Ben Davis quotes a Culture Track study which affirms: 'For today's audiences, the definition of culture has democratized, nearly to the point of extinction. It's no longer about high versus low or culture versus entertainment; it's about relevance or irrelevance. Activities that have traditionally been considered culture and those that haven't are now on a level playing field.' That means a 'trashy' social media-oriented space like the Museum of Ice Cream, that charges $40 for entry and has queues snaking down the street, can become more relevant in today's culture than something traditionally cultural, like the Museum of Modern Art.

Attaining relevance to the moment is a significant part of what it means to build a brand (and remember, today everything is a brand from a restaurant to an individual). Relevance is not achieved via old-school notions of emotional inception. Instead, it happens through cultural imprinting. Cultural imprinting is 'the mechanism whereby an ad changes the landscape of current culture rather than trying to change our minds individually. In changing the cultural landscape, it changes how we are perceived by others when we use a brand's products.'[1]

OFFLINE BEATS ONLINE

To change the cultural landscape, the adverts and actions of a brand need to be public. This means that offline activities achieve cultural imprinting in ways that online ads and experiences cannot. We need to see them and know – or be able to assume – that everyone else has too. Online ads are targeted and social feeds are assembled by algorithms and data that is unique to each person, so I don't know what you've seen and likely don't receive the same ads as you. As computer scientist and philosophy writer Jaron Lanier explains:

Algorithms choose what each person experiences through their devices. This component might be called a feed, a recommendation engine, or personalisation. It means each person sees different things. The immediate motivation is to deliver stimuli for individualised behaviour modification.[2]

Offline creations build the culture that surrounds us. Poster campaigns, billboards, outdoor takeovers, 'city attacks', hyped parties, open events – these are all places where cultural imprinting happens. Studies by (scary) social media listening agency Engagement Labs found that: 'There is little to no relationship between the conversations happening on social media versus those that happen in real life'.[3] Marketing correspondent Samuel Scott aptly adds: 'The digital world is not the real world. I remember ads I saw on TV 20 years ago. I do not remember blog spam or display or social media ads that I saw yesterday.'[4]

Do you remember the iPod ads? It was 2002 and iPod adverts were everywhere you turned. They dominated billboards and prime time TV slots. They danced on the pre-rolls at the cinema. The colourful posters with silhouettes were splashed all across the city and on the pages of newspapers. We didn't know what it was, but it felt like something you should know about. iPods were lively, fun, and the future – and they were culturally imprinting. Music was to be listened on-the-go, and the internet and digitisation made unprecedented access to it now possible. Apple spent tens of millions of dollars on mass media to advertise the iPod globally. There were hundreds of millions of people around the world who were exposed to Apple's advertising, who had absolutely no prior knowledge of, or interest in, an iPod.

Today's advertising agencies would call those enormous amounts of money spent on untargeted efforts a 'waste'. They were marketing iPods to the uninterested. But were they?

Far from waste, what makes ads important and determining of success is the very fact that people besides the targets see them.[§] Who bought an iPod, and how explosive was it for the imprint of Apple as a brand? And most notably, how many of us went on to have another handheld Apple device, the iPhone?

CHECK MY RELEVANCE

We like to visibly associate ourselves with what's relevant. What a product, service, or activity 'says' about you only matters if people see you using it. Clothes, drinks, cars, cafés, phones – these things send cultural signals. That TV show you've seen and talked about at work, that brand of soap in your bathroom when friends come over. What is used and consumed in public is what shapes our cultural landscape. With social media we can take the private and make it public. But to get to this point we first have to want to be associated with the cultural signals that the brand images allow us to send. The online promotion is a result of the offline imprint. The offline impression is the gateway to potential dissemination online.

RELEVANCE LIVES OFFLINE

Our offline surroundings, people, and conversations are the cues that show us what is culturally relevant. This is where the dialogue of the zeitgeist happens – and where we get in on it. Cultural imprinting is the mechanic for relevance that gets brands/organisations/people/movements into consensus reality, and thus become part of the cultural landscape.

So, what to do? Poster a city instead of buying online banners. Throw an event rather than paying for a social campaign! Get over 'influencers' and prioritise face time with an audience you care about. Empathise. Question. Make art and call it marketing. Make marketing that gets mistaken for art. Earn respect. Build an altruistic space within the cultural landscape. Focus on offline and enter the dialogue of what's relevant.

[§]   DIGITAL MARKETING OVERLOOKS SIGNALLING IN ITS PREOCCUPATION WITH TARGETING. THEY SAY THAT TARGETABILITY IS THE KEY ATTRIBUTE THEY SEEK FROM AN ADVERTISING MEDIUM, BUT IT IS MASS SIGNALLING NOT MASS MEDIA THAT BUILDS BRANDS.

OVER CONTENT CREATION
Putting the Audience Before Yourself

SCREEN LIFE

Today we spend an average of nine hours a day in front of screens. Minimum. This includes your computer at work, your TV at home, and your mobile phone for all those times in between (or simultaneously). These devices conspire to drain our attention, attention that could be given to doing all those things we 'can never find the time for'. Oh, the delight of life in the 'attention economy'. These two words have become highly familiar by now. They signal that human attention has become a resource, a currency growing in value as it becomes increasingly scarce. In post-industrial societies, attention spans have become the engine of the economy.

Every business is an engine fuelled by attention. In the farms and fields of primitive societies, and in the factories of the Industrial Revolution, physical manpower drove the economy. In the information era, knowledge was power – the more a company had, the more successful it could be. But now, as flows of unnecessary information clog workers' brains and corporate communication links, attention is the rare resource that truly powers a company.[1]

The attention economy turns our attention into a form of labour, and consequently into a new means of capitalist exploitation. Our attention is captured via the complex algorithms and behaviour-modifying designs of platforms, apps and websites. They serve up 'engaging' content, collect data to sell, and constantly find new ways of keeping us in environments where we can be sold to. These mechanisms are both deliberate and deceptive, designed specifically to keep us glued there.

Like clean air, attention is something that once could be had for free but is now being encroached upon as the next and perhaps final frontier.[2]

JONATHAN BELLER

Jaron Lanier, referring to these behaviour-modifying platforms as 'BUMMERs', describes them as machines composed of six moving parts.[§] 'Attention-acquisition' is one, as is surveillance, data-tracking, and 'cramming content down your throat' by way of feeds and recommendation engines, including content from third parties. Lanier reckons:

The [above] elements are connected to create a measurement and feedback machine that deliberately modifies behaviour. The process runs thus: customised feeds become optimised to 'engage' each user, often with emotionally potent cues, leading to addiction. People don't realise how they are being manipulated. The default purpose of manipulation is to get people more and more glued in, and to get them to spend more and more time in the system.[‡3]

A NON-COMPELLING CONTRADICTION

The cognitive labour involved in the attention economy places the creative worker smack bang in the middle of it. Who makes the content used to gather the attention? Us. Who is the consumer of content? Also us. We are both producers and consumers, those who supply and those who demand. We have experienced both sides of the exchange. We know what it takes to craft 'engaging' content and we know how it feels to watch brand campaigns, observe promoted posts, receive newsletters, close pop-ups, and read sponsored articles. We can instantly recognise that icky feeling after losing 30 minutes scrolling through a feed. We can identify the 'how did that happen?' moment in an instant. I went on to check a message and somehow found myself doing a quick browse of a clothing boutique's new arrivals. The 'how did I get here?' snap is one thing. The feel-bad effect is another.

No matter how brief and mild, sadness is the default mental state of the online billions...

After checking for the tenth time what someone said on Instagram, the pain of the social makes us feel miserable, and we put the phone away.[‡4]   GEERT LOVINK

[§]   BUMMER STANDS FOR 'BEHAVIOURS OF USERS MODIFIED AND MADE INTO AN EMPIRE FOR RENT'. THE ACRONYM WAS CREATED BY LANIER TO DESCRIBE SOCIAL MEDIA PLATFORMS, WHICH NEED US TO KEEP COMING BACK SO THEY HAVE ENGINEERED THEIR DESIGNS TO MANIPULATE US INTO DOING SO. THEY ACCUMULATE DATA ABOUT US, THEN RETURN WITH MORE OF WHAT MOVES US MOST TO GENERATE WEALTH FOR THEMSELVES. LANIER'S PERSPECTIVE IS THAT BUMMER PLATFORMS ARE MORE THAN JUST A BUMMER – THEY'RE ERODING HEALTH AND HAPPINESS, OBSCURING THE TRUTH, AND IMPACTING OUR CAPABILITY TO EMPATHISE.

The creative industries pour their labour into digital content creation for the purpose of advertising, promotion, selling, and overall attention-seeking. The general motivation could be summarised as: 'We want you to know about everything we deem important. We will capture your attention, irrespective of where you would prefer to hold it.' That is the main objective of the brand or organisation. Regardless of whether that is 'we want you to know we have this great sale on', or 'we want you to know about our latest exhibition' – it's all the same. This supposedly significant communication takes the form of video spots, animations, advertorials, product tie-ins... an array of shapes and sizes fit to any situation or environment. On the production side is an intense degree of pressure to 'create content', a deluge of low-quality, attention-sucking drivel, there to blanket us from the meaningful things in life. In a word, distraction. Very little of this content is valuable. Very little of it is worth what we exchange for it: our time, concentration, mental health, social connections, and bio-equilibriums – to offer just a short list. Content has become synonymous with digital information, from images and videos to articles and podcasts. These often take forms that mask their true nature as advertising. Camouflaged as legitimate journalism, for instance, they distort the viewer's ability to discern when they are looking at something commercial.

'Engaging content' is a term used for the net to catch attention. For designers, writers, programmers, and all sorts of other creative professionals, this is a brief you will receive again and again. It will typically come with a requirement to highlight the client's do-gooder credentials, like being 'committed to impacting the lives of today's youth'. The masses on social media are a tempting channel for such a brief. This is a captive audience, a sea of wide eyes around the world, hypnotised and waiting for flashing posts and numbing information. Yet using social media to communicate with an audience is an automatic dismissal of respect for their life experience. The use of platforms, data, and mechanisms designed to manipulate the behaviour and emotions of the receiver means that the relationship is exploitative from day one. It is a clear contradiction to claim care via attention-abusing means.

We point fingers at the platforms for their damaging influence, for invading our privacy and playing with our emotions – but those buying the advertising communications are equally complicit in these effects. If you are putting your content there, you are equally to blame. Who is taking a stance to *not* be where these detrimental effects are caused? Talking ethics sounds moralistic. How about a simple acknowledgement of another's quality of life? If you care about your audience's wellbeing, not using social media is a no-brainer. As Nadia

Idle says, with biting clarity: 'Cycling between vacuous, hysterical hedonism and pitiful illness is not my idea of the good life. Witnessing loved ones descend into this is also not my idea of the good life.'[+5]

YOUR CONTENT
IS THE CAUSE

Is all commercial content deployed with malice? I suspect many are simply imitating what they see around them. This is what everyone else is doing, so it must be the way things are done. Classic conformist behaviour. These clients commissioning creative work (or perhaps even your boss) are thinking 'where else would I tell my story?' whilst reading boilerplate 'Social Media Best Practice' drivel and blindly following whatever it says. They are unaware that they too are being played by the same advertising machines.

The problem isn't any particular technology, but the use of technology to manipulate people, to concentrate power in a way that is so nuts and creepy that it becomes a threat to the survival of civilisation.[+6]   JARON LANIER

CONTENT OR DISCONTENT?

Like many, you wish your work would have a positive impact on the world. Maybe you've noted the degradation of our longstanding social connections, the fact that strangers no longer interact with one another, or our total lack of recognition for others as we walk like zombies through the city, heads hanging over glowing screens. Brainwashed by the Cult of Digital. Eyes glazed over. Scrolling morbidly. Is this something that disturbs you? If only there was something to be done...
Here lies the question. What is 'content creation' doing to people? We know the answer and nobody is confronting it. Can we really place hope in a Silicon Valley 'humane tech' movement? Active in the creative industries, the rabid technosolutionism of social media

is exacerbating everything we lament about our lives. And yet we sense no possibility for alternatives. What about creativity that lives *offline*? What about ways to connect with people that do not engage in behaviour modification and play on negative emotions? There are other approaches that could facilitate healthier experiences for an audience. There are different strategies that promote getting together in person, interacting, socialising, looking each other in the eye, and decompressing from our incessant digital demands. Take a radical reexamination of what's at stake and question the 'prove it with metrics' requirement. Be an advocate for getting off your phone and out into the world. Take an active role in your future, gifting yourself time to properly consider your dreams and desires.

Think this sounds impossible? Believe that conscientiousness is dead and it is all too good to be true? Fear not, it's happening. There are game-changers out there. Groove Therapy is one. It is a dance school in Australia started by Vanessa Marian. Vanessa is a dancer and choreographer, and she wanted to start beginner dance classes for adults that were not intimidating and helped build community. To reduce any reservations, they have a 'no mirrors, dim lights' policy. 'We run weekly adult dance classes for the everyday person and funnel the profits from this into our community outreach dance projects', they assert, 'So yes, you are legit doing a good deed by taking class with us'.

In an announcement of radical conscientiousness, Marian explained:

The new financial year has marked a new chapter for us, and we really sat down as a fam to think about who we are, what we stand for and how we will push harder to champion this at Groove Therapy. We have made some executive decisions and some changes - both big and small - and it's all centred around our ideas on the meaning of life.

More focus on mental wellness, less focus on social media.

We told a marketing expert at a billion-dollar social enterprise that we wanted to cut down on social media marketing and his response was a big cringe face, followed by a 'WHOA. Congrats on sticking to your morals, you brave things...' Creating the meaningful means quality over quantity, so expect to see less of us on your feed, but with way more depth.

This was the first time I had seen this level of consideration from a company towards their content output. It demonstrated a notable degree of self-awareness, calling to mind the subtitle of counter-cultural economist EF Schumacher's largely forgotten work *Small is Beautiful (1973) – 'Economics As If People Mattered'*. As if people mattered, this

care and consideration was significant and deserving of recognition. I sent them a note of commendation. They responded:
This is the kind of thing that makes our decision seem less scary! So glad it resonates with you. It means a lot.

DO NOT BE DISCOURAGED

Being non-conformist *is* scary. Trying to move outside the norm is not easy. Leading means looking around and seeing no one beside you – it's a lonely place to be out front! But this is exactly what it's about. Doing what no one else is doing, because it feels right. The platforms aren't going to help us spend less time at our screens. We can act and unleashing this action on the cult of mindless content creation is a sign of where to start.

OBSCURED   PERSUASION
Vigilance Against Covert Marketing

Find ways to get products in front of people without them realising they're being persuaded to buy them. That's the goal. Covert marketing, undercover marketing, embedded marketing, content marketing, native advertising, brand journalism... all of these are names for one of marketing's favourite tricks – by no means new, but given a whole new, shareably devious lease on life thanks to social media. These are ads sculpted to reduce a consumer's ad recognition by blending into an existing environment, like news websites, search results, or podcast streams. Their cunning stealthiness gets sharper by the day. These ads-in-disguise are sneaking through all sorts of former barriers.

You too would have noted the increased popularity of a style of email newsletter I call the 'Link List'.[§] It's just that, a 'curated' list of links that the newsletter's creator decides to share with their readers. Besides Link Lists becoming a trend in themselves, another trend has emerged that demonstrates just how good stealth marketing has gotten – the unintentional inclusion of articles in these lists that are of an advertising nature rather than genuinely editorial. They look so similar to regular articles that they are able to make it onto these suggested reading lists, unbeknownst to their compilers.[§§] How remarkable – even ad industry insiders cannot differentiate what is and what isn't advertising anymore.

A BIG HIT ACROSS ALL CORNERS OF THE CREATIVITY-AS-WORK SPHERE.   [§]

AN ARTICLE TITLED 'LIFE WITHOUT THE IPHONE IS PRETTY DAMN GREAT' WAS   [§§]
INCLUDED IN A LINK LIST, AND SOUNDS LIKE A TYPICAL, POPULAR ADDRESS
OF DIGITAL MINIMALISM AND ITS LIFE-CHANGING CAPABILITIES. ON CLOSER
INSPECTION THE PIECE OPENLY SLAMS APPLE, WHILE GUSHING OVER GOOGLE AND ITS
PIXEL PHONE. RATHER THAN A TREATISE ON RECOVERY FROM SMARTPHONE-ADDICTION,
THE ARTICLE IS SPONSORED CONTENT.

DEEPER AND DEEPER UNDERCOVER

As native advertising[§] and content marketing becomes more covert, it gets harder to distinguish true journalism from a sales message veiled in story. Discerning content marketing from editorial content is increasingly difficult. Advertisers and publishers try to obscure the fact that it's an ad as much as possible, hiding a tiny 'sponsored by...' at the bottom of the page or having no visible sign at all. Regulation around this is still in its infancy and varies massively between regions. The sad part is, media outlets have compromised their genuine editorial content by giving way to advertisers.[§§] Once trusted sources for unbiased opinion and quality journalism, they are now heavily peppered with sponsored content that blurs the line between their genuine work and pieces of advertising. It's the fastest growing form of advertising. And it doesn't appear to be slowing.

AN   ALL   NEW   GAME   OF
TRUE   OR   FALSE

SO WHAT? MAYBE THIS BEATS TRAD AD

Naturally, many practitioners argue that these new types of advertising are an improvement over other forms because:

A. (In theory) We receive advertising for things relevant to us rather than irrelevant commercial clutter.

And B. It's less intrusive than traditional marketing messages because we do not have to stop to interact with it. It occurs in the flow of our day.

[§] 'NATIVE ADVERTISING' IS ADVERTISING THAT BLENDS INTO THE ENVIRONMENT WHERE IT APPEARS. THESE ENVIRONMENTS WILL BE PLACES WITH A PREEXISTING LEVEL OF TRUST FROM THE CONSUMER (E.G. A VIDEO PRODUCER WHOM WE ALREADY FOLLOW) THAT THE ADVERTISER PAYS TO GET IN ON. IT IS DELIBERATELY AMBIGUOUS IN NATURE AND DIFFICULT TO IDENTIFY.

[§§] MEDIA OUTLETS HAVE THEIR OWN PAID-CONTENT DEPARTMENTS DEDICATED TO COVERT MARKETING. TAKE THE GLOBALLY REVERED NEW YORK TIMES. NYT NOW HAS T BRAND STUDIO, THEIR DEPARTMENT MADE UP OF TRAINED JOURNALISTS, PURELY DEDICATED TO THE CREATION OF SPONSORED CONTENT. T BRAND STUDIO IS THE BRAND MARKETING UNIT OF THE NEW YORK TIMES. 'WE CREATE CONTENT AND EXPERIENCES THAT SPARK IMAGINATION AND INFLUENCE THE INFLUENTIAL.'

The costs for both consumers and society as a whole far outweigh these 'benefits'. The traditional line between 'church and state' (editorial content and advertising) has virtually disappeared, and with it the symbolic cues that enable us to know when we are interacting with advertising. 'Sharing' puts focus on our personal relationships and lets marketeers monetise our friendships. And as companies become more adept at data collection and analytics, it's corporations who control what we see. Because content production is driven by the tracking of data, popularity determines what gets published and supported. In essence, this means an equal playing field is gone. Instead of artistic talent or unaffected information standing before the electorate, likes, shares and followers become the currency of importance.

In his book *Bad Men*, advertising industry veteran Bob Hoffman states: 'One of the most harmful effects of digital media is the way they have blurred the line between fact and fiction. The marketing industry has been at the forefront of this, using various techniques to fool consumers.' He highlights Google as the leader in deception, describing their mission for maximum blurring of these lines. 'Google makes its money by misdirection. They're geniuses at it. When you type a phrase in their search box, the first results you get are all ads, not natural search results.' Google ads used to have defined borders or backgrounds in different colours (still there in 2013), but have become increasingly indistinguishable over time.

The message is be alert. Be on high awareness for marketing in all its perverse forms. Put pressure on your favoured media outlets to be transparent. Consider that subscription-based publishers might be charging fees as part of the struggle to keep real. Be discerning and observant before you send an 'article' to a friend or repost advertising.

FORMER GHOST WRITER

One of my past lives in creative work was as a ghost writer for one of the world's most successful rappers. I would write pages of quotes and full-length interviews, putting words in the mouth of this guy. These were sent over to his 'team', who would then return the ones 'approved' for PR use. Despite never meeting the man, it didn't take long to see what style and tone they preferred. I read up on his interviews (probably penned by other ghost writers, though possibly transcribed from the horse's mouth) and studied his social accounts. A key part of the job was to subtly insert nods to a certain collaboration with a brand, and explain elements of that project with scientific details that were sufficiently vague. I soon found a formula for meeting this goal in a convincing manner. My hit rate for 'approved' work went up and up. Soon I was receiving interview questions straight from magazines and news outlets looking to speak to Mr ███████████████████. I could turn these around within hours, effectively generating high-value PR for both the rapper and the brand at very low cost (I was not well paid). It was fun and weird work (imagine filling in interviews for this guy for Italian Rolling Stone and Mexican GQ magazines), that gave me great leverage for a substantial pay rise that year. Thanks to Excel sheets I found documenting estimates of this generated PR value, I had hard numbers that dwarfed my meagre salary. Earning tactics aside, this process gave me insight into how lifestyle articles are infused with deception and dishonesty. Marketing and online content are deeply entangled. Virtually nothing can be taken at face value when the media scene is this polluted.

MARKETING NEEDN'T BE COVERT

Aren't these procedures to 'invisibly' integrate a marketing message or brand acknowledgement into an environment kind of pathetic? There is a cowardliness about it. With advertising, and particularly the online type, comes a consistent sour taste of zero nobility. Could you not come up with something you were proud to put your name to? A form of promotion that wasn't attempting to deceive? When explaining this tactical obscuring of motive to somebody who doesn't work in marketing, they replied with something simple and true:

Why are marketeers trying to hide it? Why not do something... ahem, creative? I resent the thought of reading an article and not knowing it was an advertisement in disguise. If I knew who was behind that, it would immediately discredit them. It would put me off buying anything from them. I would no longer trust the news outlet.

Does this tactic actually work? It sounds like a turnoff.

NEVER   NOT   OBSCURING

MAX   DECEIT   GUARANTEED!

Hiding messaging into so-called 'content' proves yet again that this unwavering dedication to digital marketing seeks little more than to manipulate the audience. It's an ungodly level of effort to apply to misleading somebody. Imagine pouring that dedication instead into a totally new idea that sought to improve, excite, care or [_____]?

When we're at the stage where we are trying to obscure our intentions, shouldn't we be questioning that intention altogether?

SHOCK	ME.	PLEASE.
Pervasive	Boring	Creativity

Who knew living a creative life would feel so arid? Where is the joy, the excitement, the risk, or the shock? Nothing is shocking besides the diminishing sense of possibility – and the working conditions. The work is safe, predictable, and supposedly 'predicted'. All conforming to predetermined directives. It's not a matter of standing out, it's a matter of fitting in and doing that very well. *Future Shock. Present Shock. The Shock of the New.* Do we even know how to feel shock anymore? I mean real shock – confused, challenging, discomfort-at-oddity shock. Not the shock we are 'supposed' to feel. Not the shock when we look around and see others acting shocked, then follow along accordingly – hazarding a guess that, because they're doing it, it ought to be done. Except, nothing is being done. What are we really doing here? What are we even creating now? More 'engaging content' to exasperate the masses, complicit in the contemporary zombie condition? More riffs on past styles, never-ending re-runs of previous cultural moments? More distractions and ever-cooler ways to say 'spend, spend, spend!' without quite saying it?

BORING.

This work is the boredom of having to come up with ideas to be 'sold in' using images of other existing creations. Mood boards, visual concept presentations, mini reels made of found footage. The client or the boss needs to see what they're paying for before it has been made.

They perceive this as low risk, a way to gain a sense of security. They know upfront exactly what they are agreeing to and what they will get. This forms a promise that is 100% based on past creations. You agree to recreate this assemblage you've shown them. To deviate in any way will be problematic, both to the project and the relationship. Creative work is boring when it's only history repeating. Whether or not originality is still possible is a separate issue. Either way, there is no possibility for it to arise in this process. And we wonder why there is nothing new anymore.

We are surrounded by worn-out, banal, useless and exhausted images, limping and dragging themselves behind the rest of our cultural evolution.[†1] WERNER HERZOG

I don't have time to make newness.

ANONYMOUS PRECARIOUS GRAPHIC DESIGNER
MARCH 2020. OVERHEARD CONVERSATION.

'Only boring people get bored' said snarky parents and teachers. A phrase that rings out with pangs of guilt. Am I boring? Boredom can be a protective barrier from the world. It's not a boredom of your deep self. It's psychic armour. These are not qualities of the individual. They manifest as barricades made from the mass celebration of mediocrity. Don't stand out, blend in. Appropriate and imitate. Only a rebellious mind will fear this state and seek to act.

NO   THRALDOM

JUST   BOREDOM

Is boredom a condition of possibility for creativity? Like the mindlessness conjured by taking a shower or a long walk. These situations seems closer to a mind free from burden or concern. Space-clearing practices. A breather for a moment away, that may just turn into an exciting moment with. Office-bound boredom, performative-process boredom, overdone-rehashings-of-predictable-ideas-and-strategies-gone-before boredom. These are the boredoms of limitation. The boredoms of 'playing it safe'. The boredoms that come from adherence to supposed certainty of result. The boredom of a decision made because *everyone else is doing it*. These are forms of boredom that are just numb anticlimax and nothing more. Weirdness has vacated the scene. There's nothing obscure. The sensation of surprise is nowhere to be found. Everything is serious. Empty of exuberance. Sorry (not sorry) to puncture the fantasy of joyful participation.

What happened to youthful rebellion, experimentation, interventions, wilful acts of destruction, the attitude to tell what sucks to fuck off, and the expressive pleasure of challenging what you dislike? Is this twee and are there ways to respond without being re-packaged back into yet another commodity for sale? Imagination and critical thought can generate forms of counter-power. The challenge is their life as a non-constitutive element in the reproduction of capital. It's about making a transgressive new propaganda ensemble. From us!

You have to keep trying to make an experiment work.
You have to keep writing this particular story,
not some story in general.[+2]

DONNA HARAWAY

On a side note – though shocking and related nonetheless – during all of this one must remember that in creativity-as-work, negativity is not allowed. *Great! Love it! So badass!!!* Be positive or be penalised. Your lack of 'spirit' will be held against you. You will be labelled a dark cloud, and nobody wants to work with a dark cloud. You're required to 'bring the good vibes' no matter what the truth is. Dissatisfaction or despair are fast tickets to the unemployment desert. Not to mention the social one. Which would you prefer: to be deserted or to keep it phoney? Who's more boring: Negative Nelly or Overly Optimistic Oli?

TIRED OF PANEL TALKS
Why This Format Has Reached Fatigue

Who hasn't attended a panel talk? Who can't picture that line up of 'influential' people on stage, the ones deemed interesting enough to gather an audience? Panel talks went from debate and discussion format to full-on marketing tool. Brands use them for 'activation', corporate sponsors as a place to be seen, and cultural entities as an opportunity to exhibit their 'discourse'. These motivations render panel talks manipulative from the get-go. An informative event is merely the lure. We are there to be seduced. For our perception of the organisers, sponsors, and speakers to be influenced.

Panel discussions have become the de-facto 'activation', the default event series, appearing like a disease at any conference or festival. Their ubiquity means that even the phrase 'panel discussion' induces an already-expectant state. Little anticipation remains, just an anticlimax followed by indifference.[§] The prospect that anything *exciting* could happen is gone. We know nothing is on the line. We know – even before we enter the room – that the entire setup only ensures what is socially permitted.

ARE WE BEATING THE HYPE OR ORGANISING IT?

Here is what will happen. The audience will sit obediently looking up at the stage as the MC of some sort poses questions and stimulates answers from their line-up of carefully *curated* 'thought-leaders'. This dynamic already posits the audience as the consumer in the room. They are there to be fed. To digest not only the conversation, but the ulterior motives surrounding it. There may be a Q&A portion after, but even then the audience's role is to eat up whatever those on stage dish out. It becomes just another life situation disguising a consumer transaction. This all sounds done to death and too dull to endure. So why do we keep coming back?

THE PANEL'S SPEED-DATING-LIKE BROTHER, THE PECHA KUCHA-STYLE PRESENTATION [§]
WHERE MANY SPEAKERS RAPID FIRE TO AN AUDIENCE, IS ANOTHER FORMAT TO REACH
THE SAME EXHAUSTION.

KNOWING BETTER BUT TEMPTED ANYWAY

Panel talks reel us in by exposing our inherent desire to get up close and personal, our increasing predilection for all-areas-access. No longer is it enough to watch the actor on screen. We want to know what they eat, see their homes, and follow their day-to-day mundanities in detail. We want to know the secret of how that self-made woman made her millions. Besides the passive, consumerist dynamic, panel talks tap into this hunger for 'bonus footage'. We are tempted by the opportunity for insider information. We want exclusive entry that won't be experienced by the masses. Is this appetite a drive for empathy and understanding, or undue curiosity? If the panel talk embodies one form of this hunger, the interview displays another. Curator Tereza Stejskalová explains:

Interviews are children of opportunity... conjuring the promise of the actual from the signs of the present.

At its core the interview is ambivalent. On the one hand, it has the potential to capture the openness of the present moment before it is subjected to the verdict of the future. On the other, the popularity of the genre across all levels of published output is also a symptom of our obsession with the present moment, our impatience, and our inability to perceive things from the perspective of a longer time horizon... The genre of the interview is determined by a tension between manipulation, conscious intention and the uncontrollable.[‡1]

We know the panel is safe. Yet for some reason we keep sitting in those chairs. Is it the promise of catching a glimpse of *something more*, the potential to get in on something early – a mere sense of FOMO if you will – that keeps the panel talk alive? Do we suffer the boredom for the small window of hope that something uncontrolled could happen?

Performative panels are obviously not about any potential spontaneity that could happen on the day, nor are they a gift to the audience. The goal is for the audience to receive a carefully predetermined message from the providers, whether it be a brand, corporation, cultural body, or the panellists themselves. This is the message behind the message. Hosting a panel of feminist activists, for example, allows a company or organisation to associate itself with the values of a movement. The so-called value of the performance is simply that it happened, that you saw it, and that photos, videos, and other media can be gathered to prove it to those who didn't attend.[§]

A DIFFERENT MOTIVATION

When considering our own creative work, how else can the audience be considered? We don't need to be spoon fed soundbites. I don't want to be a promo-pic outcome of somebody's 'content creation' plan. We don't need to get more content drivel for our eyes to receive and glaze over. We require more opportunities to activate. What would happen if we start from the motivation to still meet face-to-face, but in a way that allows the audience to be active rather than passive? Less observer, more fire-starter. Less safe content-making, more experimentation. If we let go of these displays of predetermined information and drop this concept that certain people are more interesting than others, could we find ourselves in a far more radical situation?

Less back-patting in a row on stage. More spontaneity and weirdness. Please.

'CONTENT CREATION' IS A COMMON DRIVER AND OBJECTIVE OF IRL EVENTS, OFTEN §
SEEN AS BEING MORE IMPORTANT THAN THE EVENT ITSELF. THE RATIONALE IS THAT
DOCUMENTATION OF THE HAPPENING IS ESSENTIAL FOR EXTENDED PROMOTION, WE
CAN NO LONGER NOT DIGITISE THE NON-DIGITAL. IT IS THOSE IN THE ROOM WHO
PAY THE PRICE FOR ITS PRIORITISATION. THE AUDIENCE AND THEIR EXPERIENCE
ARE SECONDARY TO THE SHOT LIST OF THE PHOTOGRAPHER, FLITTERING AROUND
AND OBSTRUCTING YOUR VIEW. THE AUDIENCE'S CONSENT IN BECOMING FUTURE
MARKETING MATERIAL IS ALSO MURKY. IS FREE ENTRY TO THE EVENT SEEN AS AUTO-
REMUNERATION FOR THIS DEAL? DID WE EVER REALLY AGREE TO BECOMING UNPAID
EXTRAS? THIS SOUNDS LIKE THAT OLD TROPE 'IF YOU'RE NOT PAYING FOR IT, THEN
YOU'RE THE PRODUCT'. I DON'T KNOW ABOUT YOU, BUT I AM NOT OVER FEELING THAT
THAT IS NOT OKAY. IT APPEARS THAT 'CONTENT CREATION' IS THE ULTERIOR MOTIVE
OF MANY OFFLINE HAPPENINGS THAT KEEP THEM STUCK IN TECHNODETERMINIST,
PSEUDO-GENEROSITY.

EVERYONE IS BORED
Everything is Boring

We are meant to relish boredom. Indulge in it like the latest luxury treatment. Even make time for it. Who has spare time, let alone for being bored? Read up on 'How To Do Nothing' they say. But aren't we bored already? Just because we are busy doesn't mean we are doing much of anything.

We find ourselves suspended between a compulsion to do too much and a wish to do nothing. The distractions of net-surfing are a kind of weird convergence of these impulses. Comparing twenty-three minor variations on a white T-shirt, consuming dozens of viral videos or scrolling through metres of social media feeds...[1]

We are all bored and everything is boring. Occupied 24/7, doing nothing at all. There is no sight more boring than someone staring at their phone. No gesture more boring than the flick, flick, flick of a scroll. No distress more boring than patting pockets. No panic more boring than 1% battery. No sound more boring than no one talking on the bus. No project more boring than self-help. No status more boring than unfinished.

There is no suggestion more boring than 'be positive'. No belief more boring than work-life balance. No status more boring than over-committed. No lie more boring than, *I'll reply later.* No habit more boring than forgetfulness. No list more boring than 'To Do'. No place more boring than a café that looks like an office. No office more boring than one trying to look like a café. No dilemma more boring than still underpaid. No diagnosis more boring than low-grade burnout. No excuse more boring than 'can't sorry, busy'. No emotion more boring than loneliness, by choice. No night more boring than a sleepless one. No worry more boring than that of tomorrow.

When I was bored as a kid, I would nag my parents for something to do. That boredom was uncomfortable and unbearable. We wanted out ASAP. We would act in an instant to escape it. This new boredom is void of energy. It doesn't cause us to complain. We're not annoyed. We just take it, accepting it as the contemporary condition. Not interrogating. Not caring.

A NEW BOREDOM.
WITH NONE OF THE IRRITATION
AND ALL OF THE DISCOMFORT.

Except, we cannot dare say we are bored – so we pretend to be busy.

FAKING BUSY

Boredom loves busy because busy masks boredom. 'Busy' is allowed, boredom is not. Busy = good. Boredom = bad. Important people are busy. To be busy is to be wanted. 'Can't sorry, I'm *sooo* busy.' To be bored is to be vacant. Sitting, waiting, wishing. Public vacancy is a risk. Your reputation as a freelancer risks being downgraded if you're not occupied. Your social status as a friend risks decline if you're easy to make plans with – to be busy is to be popular. Scarcity 101. Parents are proud of busy kids. With busyness as a status symbol, we start to fake it.

Too tired to go out. 'Not tonight sorry, I'm busy.' Besides, we are told it's important to make time to *do nothing*. Stay home, binge-watch a series. 'Self-care'. Late night scroll. Boring.

Work sucks but I can prop up a pleasant façade with tactics of busyness. I'll block my calendar so I appear to be in meetings. Disappearance is key to importance-management (the more important you are, the less you're around). I finish what I have to do quickly, then use the office printer for my personal projects. Paper doubles as a prop for busyness. Sometimes I send an email late at night to look like I'm *really* applying myself.

Pretending to be busy is the performance of our lives. We act how we want to come across while we watch from the wings, sitting in dull darkness. Sitting in the wings is uneventful. A boring display of ourselves performs before us.

WE   ARE   ALL   BORED,
AND   NOBODY   CARES

TOO BUSY TO FEEL

We are as numbed by the busyness performance as we are the boredom. The busyness is as hypnotic as the boring. Constant 'doing' muddles with the always-bored. There are no borders. 'Distraction provides the only relief from a perpetually incomplete to-do list. Not working becomes at least as tiring and incessant as working.' [2]

Tiring and incessant, or dull? We're supposed to be fulfilled by work, but work's no fun. Taking time off to refresh doesn't help. It only invites guilt about not working. A guilt that 'relaxation' cannot shake. Friends are another to-do, and let's not start with family. They will always be there anyway. Romance took a back seat to being ready for an early start. Who am I kidding? I'm not sleeping. But I can maintain tasks related to appearance, physical and otherwise. Looking good matters. It's all a matter of looking good.

Life gets linear, flattens out. No peaks or troughs. Just a monotonous hum of uninteresting apprehension. It's a tranquillity not composed of stillness but restlessness. A restlessness that drives towards the perpetual hustle of simple distractions. Too tired for action, too wound-up to decompress. I'll float here somewhere in-between, inert but convincing myself *something* will happen eventually.

We are nervous of pressing the off switch on our machines and minds, as though fearing the void that may be made visible. [3]

Exhausted but bored. Exploited but grateful. Determined but distracted. Multi-tasking but burning out. We know the void. We bounce between its two sides. We live in the void. Our lives *are* the void. These are the contradictions that form its walls, that create the depth we try to fill. A consciously futile activity. This preoccupation provides no reprieve but at least denies any pain.

HOW TO BREAK
THE HYPNOSIS?

WHAT COULD RUPTURE
THE MONOTONY
OF BORED-BUT-BUSY?

EVERYDAY SURREALISM.
A PRANK.
A CHALLENGE.
AN UNEXPLAINABLE
STRANGENESS.
ANYTHING ABSURD.
ANYTHING
WITHOUT REASON.

FAKE   BUSY

Nobody   Wants   To   Be   Vacant

Faking being busy at work. Faking being busy with friends. Pretending to be busy to our families. Using it with dates. Performing busyness with ourselves, creating distractions from the void of despair. Or, feeling so deeply bound to the guilt of productivity that leisure time becomes an impossibility. The busyness that was once an act is now a condition.[§]

TOO   BUSY
TO   CARE

A SOCIETY OF BUSY

Overwork is a source of pride and symbol of success. A leisurely lifestyle is certainly less valued than one that is hardcore, fast-paced, non-stop, and as-much-as-possible. 'Live fast and die young.' What was once the chant of rebels, now belongs to the busy. In our culture, busyness is equated with competence and ambition. It is how we display our scarcity and market demand. We are but human capital, and these are the characteristics that capital values.

In our culture, being overworked is far better than being underworked. This perverse logic means that busyness is more than a consequence, it is a tactic for survival. If you're not visibly busy, you must be doing something wrong. You are undesirable to the market. If you were of higher value, you would be occupied and hard to get hold

[§]   WHEN WE'RE NOT BUSY CREATING, WE'RE BUSY CONSUMING.
'OUR PERPETUAL BUSYNESS IS FUELLED BY A CULTURE THAT DERIDES OR TRIVIALIZES THE NEED TO STOP… OUR DISCOMFORT WITH STOPPING, WITH TIME UNFULFILLED AND UNSPOKEN FOR, ALSO GIVES RISE TO A MODE OF CONSTANT DISTRACTION, THE PERFECT TWIN OF THE IMPERATIVE TO WORK AND PRODUCE: THE MOMENT WE COME TO THE LIMIT OF OUR CAPACITY AS PRODUCERS, WE CAN ACTIVATE OUR CAPACITY AS CONSUMERS.' – JOSH COHEN IN NOT WORKING (2019)

of. Keeping up an image of busyness and scarce availability has become a central strategy for getting work, keeping work, and ascending the promotional ladder. A subject that is hard-to-get is highly prized.

CAN'T SORRY.

.

BUSY.

REPUTATION MANAGERS

Busyness for reputation management is a skill. It's a subtle balancing act. Too busy and you look like an underpaid hustler, the sucker of the busyness spectrum. Not busy enough and you must be mediocre. An experienced busyness-player will deploy strategies found in the dating sphere, where availability and scarcity have been manipulated since the beginning of time. 'Treat 'em mean, keep 'em keen' is as effective with employers as (we believe) it is with prospective mates.

Overwork culture and its values have become pervasive, expanding far past the traditional workspace. Society today reveres a busy person. As in the business world, busyness is valued in social scenes. The 'too-busy-to-get-hold-ofs' are sexy members of society, an exclusive club of 'red-hot-wanteds'. We like association with success. Now friends play 'hard to get' with each other to assert their status of being in-demand and highly sought-after. Are we managing our relationships like we are managing our careers? We've designed the versions of ourselves we want the world to perceive. First we perfected them for work, now we deploy them amongst friends. Social media taught us fantastic behaviours for expert image management and normalised them for broad spectrum use. The praise for always-on, upheld by common devotions to productivity, has us playing 'I'm sooooo busy' with our friends as much as potential clients. Regardless of being genuinely busy or not, busyness works as the ultimate excuse. It gets points for signalling importance and is socially accepted. In prized overwork culture and times of precarity, 'too busy' is the permissible or even admirable excuse.

STATUS SIGNALLING

'I'm so busy' could be the status signal of our time. Its products are the ear buds, the power banks, the multiple phones, the organisational apps – all the gadgets necessary for never-not-working. A fully equipped office on the go. Work anytime, anywhere. And when you're not working, status signal by keeping your headphones in. It's great getting the checkout man to not talk to you without having to say a thing.[§] Your busy-tools allow every minute to be utilisable. Don't just stand there while commuting to work, listen to an informative podcast. Maximum productivity is a possibility, priority, and becomes a point of pride.[§§] To project an image of productivity means you're industrious. You have the cleverness it takes to make the most of every minute available. In the book *Entreprecariat*, Silvio Lorusso explains:

Productivity is the aesthetic dimension of the work ethic: it is measured to increase efficiency but also to materialize one's own busyness, thus demonstrating to oneself and to others that one is occupied. Why repeat to each other the obsessive refrain of 'I don't have time'? Because... busyness is no longer just a moral imperative ('Waste of time is thus the first and in principle the deadliest of sins' said Max Weber) but it is also a status symbol, a form of economic positioning that is the reversal of Veblen's traditional leisure: today, being wealthy does not mean having more free time, but being more overburdened.[‡1]

BETTER THAN NOTHING?

Busyness took over from leisure and relaxation as the status to aim for. Remember when an aspirational life was advertised as one of wealth, relaxing by the pool or taking long drives in a convertible, wearing impractically beautiful clothes, and with jewellery and time for days? The visible landscape of an imposed aspirational life has changed

§   73% OF ADULTS AGED 18-34 ADMITTED TO HAVING SLID A PAIR OF HEADPHONES ON TO 'AVOID INTERACTION WITH OTHER PEOPLE'. (IN A SURVEY BY MUSIC LIFESTYLE BRAND SOL REPUBLIC, 2014)

§§   IN HIS BOOK *NOT WORKING* (2019), JOSH COHEN GIVES US SOME BACKGROUND UNDERSTANDING ON HOW THIS CAME TO BE:
'IN OUR CULTURE OF OVERWORK AND HYPERACTIVITY, BEING BUSY, AND BEING SEEN TO BE BUSY, HAVE BECOME THE ULTIMATE SOURCE OF OUR PRIDE AND MEANING... IN HIS SEMINAL 1905 TRACT, THE PROTESTANT ETHIC AND THE SPIRIT OF CAPITALISM, THE GERMAN SOCIOLOGIST MAX WEBER SUGGESTED THAT PROTESTANT MOVEMENTS SUCH AS LUTHERANISM AND CALVINISM HAD ENTRENCHED A KIND OF SACRALISATION OF WORK IN WESTERN SOCIETIES. THESE MOVEMENTS ENJOINED PEOPLE TO THE MOST EFFICIENT AND THRIFTY USE OF THEIR TIME IN ORDER TO MAXIMISE PRODUCTIVITY. ON THIS VIEW, THE MOST EGREGIOUS SIN IS TO IDLE, MEANDER OR STRAY, ESPECIALLY INTO ACTIVITIES – OR INACTIVITY – THAT HAVE NO DISCERNIBLE PROFIT OR PURPOSE.'

to adverts depicting 'successful' workers who, rather than having an abundance of leisure to their wealth, are time-deprived and valued for it. Slick, important, and powerful – far from haggard, these admirable individuals are 'making it'. Don't pity them. Busyness is brilliance. Ads acknowledge their missions and the degree to which these figures are time-stricken. They stand ready and waiting, offering an abundance of products and services to make these lives easier. The Wall Street Journal's 2016 campaign featured celebrities talking about their busy, busy worlds, all underscored by their key slogan: 'People who don't have time make time to read the WSJ.'

STILL   NOT   LOVING
WORKAHOLISM

BUSYNESS.FM

Lamenting 'crazy schedules' or 'desperately needing a vacation' are the soundscape of busyness as status. Non-brags are the songs and guiltlessness the station. To be deficient in leisure-time is not an embarrassment, it is a sign you are living right.

'How are you?' – the simplest question we ask one another – is now as commonly answered with 'busy!' as it was with a flat, thoughtless 'good'. This busyness is virtually never assumed to mean anything other than busy with paid work. Of course, we could be busy with household tasks or something more hedonistic in nature. But it is safe to assume the unspoken subtext is work-work. We indicate this life well lived at every opportunity because it shows we are ethical people. The role of 'hard work' is key in making us a 'good person'. Paid work is tightly bound to right life. Busy = good and virtuous. Not busy = lazy, slacker, unwanted.

ME: *Hi Nana, how are you?*

GRANDMOTHER: *I'm keeping myself busy.*

DECEMBER 2019. PHONE CALL.

OPTING OUT IS NOT AN OPTION

If you refuse to see busyness as cool, you do not get a welcome. Being critical of the busyness status means you might be inadequate to it, and thus, became anti. If you *could* function within it you would. Clearly, you can't find enough work or you aren't popular with friends. If you were ambitious you would have a drive to create constant side projects. If you were *creative* you wouldn't choose not to create as much as possible. If you're not trying to be busy, there must be something wrong. As one study noted, '...people dread idleness and desire busyness in search of meaning and motivation in their lives.'[‡2]

Under the hypnosis of living correctly, busyness bleeds from performance to reality and back again. It gets used for status and provides the perfect cover for the inner turmoil of precarious worker-life. This unique form of turmoil combines *coulds* ('I could be working later tonight', 'I could be working on a side project, too', 'I could do a diving course at night', 'I could reach out to that person and ask to start a magazine together') with *shoulds* ('I should reply to that email', 'I should write a new post', 'I should update my portfolio', 'I should be applying for more grants', 'I should take up oil painting') into a muddled never-ending despair. Surrounded by busyness propaganda, we find ourselves pressed by that inescapable next question: am I busy *enough*? The safe answer is irrespective of fact. Either way, just pretend to be.

Faking busy gets murky when you can no longer tell if it is automatic, inflicted, or by choice. The things one has to, could do, and should do provide an infinite array of possibilities to *do*, all unfolding under an environment that encourages that always-on mindset. If you cannot tell and are unsure, it's okay. Just keep running.

THINGS I HAVE TO DO
vs.   THINGS I 'HAVE TO DO'

Pretending to be busy on all fronts, from the office to the book club, is the most exhausting of performances. Real or fake, being busy is boring. 'Busy' people are boring.[§] Who is proud to decline invites with 'ugh, so busy atm!' (besides everyone) and then stay home alone? We sit by ourselves with our screens and label it 'self-care'. We're all pretending to be busy when in reality, we're burnt out and bored.[§§] So why not cut the bull, stop status signalling each other, and assess what's really at stake here?

Do we actually believe it is cool to be constantly occupied? Does it fill one with pride to say 'I'm busy'? Would you rather not, but can't understand why there is always so much to do? Can we identify the deeper compulsion that is happening? Are priorities misaligned? Can you separate the things you have to do from the things you might be choosing to 'have to do'? How much of the complicated life is being chosen and what sacrifices would make it simpler? We demote time together and ignore one another – to do what exactly? What are we so busy with? Is there another way of life we would prefer than adhering to the busyness regime?

A WISE MAN: *'You're very busy? I'm so sorry to hear that.'*

JANUARY 2020. OVERHEARD CONVERSATION.

BUSY BY CHOICE?

MAKE TWO LISTS

THINGS I HAVE TO DO:

....

....

....

....

THINGS I 'HAVE TO DO':

....

....

....

....

'I'M SO BUSY IT'S HARD TO FIND THE TIME TO TELL THAT TO PEOPLE' SHE SAID.   §

ONCE WE ACKNOWLEDGE HOW BORED WE ARE WITH BEING BUSY, THE BUSYNESS GETS   §§
LESSENED. BUSYNESS CAN SELF-DISSOLVE. IS THIS THE 'SECRET TO LESS'? THE
LESSON TO LESSEN THAT PEOPLE BUY SELF-HELP BOOKS TO FIND? THE ADMISSION
OF HAVING NO DESIRE FOR INCESSANT BUSYNESS COULD BE THE KEY. A REVOLT THAT
EMBRACES THE RIGHT TO QUESTION WHAT'S PRODUCTIVE, FEASIBLE, REALISTIC, AND
OF PERSONAL PRIORITY. AND THE RIGHT TO DO NONE OF THAT AT ALL.

ANECDOTES   FROM

PERFORMATIVE BUSYNESS AT WORK

'The best busy I've played is with bosses. They do it, so why not do it back? One can get very good at pretending to be working when in fact you're doing a personal admin task at your desk... or just killing time. Of course, there is the boring version of this, which is going on Facebook during working hours. Yawn. Why not make your "against from within" more exciting? Research ideas for passive incomes, listen to a whole album uninterrupted, correspond with a secret admirer... this is how I resist and protest, on full pay.'

'When the creative director uses absence as a display of authority (important people are allowed to come and go as they please without informing where they are going or when they'll be back), I use their absence as an opportunity. It's a balance between your conscience and your defence. When you know you're getting done what you're there to do, power to you to make use of everything around it.'

'Faking busy at work is different than in private. Performative busyness towards friends and family is stickier than towards employers. Stickier because it leans closer to exercises of power, rather than empowerment. Busyness isn't status. It's strategy.'

'A laptop can be a chain to work and tool for out-of-hours exploitation, but it is also a central tool to performative busyness. If you're behind it, you can be considered legitimately working. The exploited becomes the exploiter. If you were to do your "concepting phase" sitting at your desk flicking through magazines, or researching out on the streets, or even with the laptop closed getting lost in deep thought – the body language of that reads as "not working". Obviously, on a laptop one could be doing an infinity of un-work-related tasks, yet it will be perceived as working without question.'

THE _____ INSIDE

PERFORMATIVE BUSYNESS IN SOCIAL LIFE

'Saying "I'm crazy busy" to your friends is a non-romantic playing hard to get. Busy is sexy, available is not.'

'Receiving "ahhhhhh sorry I haven't replied – I've been so busy" is my worst but I do it too.'

'Today, one must be "on it", always. This means side projects, important work, lots of social engagements... actually seeing your friends becomes less regular, since they know you're busy and they will still be there when you're "free". You're a person who has a lot going on and at the end of the day, they know you care. There is still that low-level constant communication: txts, comments, voice messages, emojis, likes. Those things acknowledge each other's existence and become the friendship's maintenance. You're not entirely absent. You're just busy'

'My parents open every phone call with an apologetic "We know you're busy..." and their voice sounds guilty. Like, they automatically think they're interrupting me. It makes me sad I've faked it so many times to get out of something, that now they are hesitant to call me.'

'Family? They just think (constant busyness) is "young people today". That it's part of our times. Because it is.'

'I refuse to be busy.'

INTERLUDE

1. GUILT-FREE EXISTENCE

No need to 'utilise' every minute of the day. Stare out the window. Do a crossword. Sleep. Amuse yourself. Disempower the nagging voice of working 24/7. Can we decouple from ongoing goal-orientation?

2. DO WE HAVE TO TALK ALL DAY LONG?

Low-level chat communication is a remarkable syphon of energy.

3. NOTIFICATIONS OFF = NO BRAINER

Would you tolerate being repeatedly tapped on the shoulder while trying to get something done? Mediate interruptions.

4. LEARN TO FLÂNEUR

Of all the interesting people you've met in your life, we can speculate with likelihood that the ones who captivated you the most – those that left a lasting impression and remain firm in your memory – are all avid flâneuses and flâneurs.

The flâneuse or flâneur was an essential figure to any street scene in 19th century France. Mega-bourgeois, flânerie was an act limited to those who could afford to wander the streets observing society with ambivalence. Stroller, lounger, saunterer, loafer... like today's less-accepted 'slacker', they were embodiments of the 'Right To Do Nothing'. A wanderer of city streets, detached from society while taking it all in. No plans. Eyes open. Give it a go. Spend no money. Carry no phone. Take to the streets and see what the day brings.

5. WHO CARES ABOUT THE AUDIENCE?

I think the truth is if you really care about the quality of somebody's life as much as you care about the quality of your own, you have it made.

EDIE WINSOR

And this is why (not) communicating through platforms designed to addict, destroy, and diminish, matters.

BRING BACK WEIRDNESS

Where did the excitement for the weird go? The sense of surprise is nowhere to be seen. As humans we have a need for strangeness. Immersed in a societal mass complex of sadness, we posit a revival of absurdity as the antidote.

'I'M A CREATIVE' IS CRINGE

When did we decide which jobs are more creative than others? Writer? Creative. Caregiver? Not creative. Illustrator? Creative. Hairdresser? Not creative. It doesn't take much thought to realise the work of a caregiver or hairdresser requires as much creativity as that of a writer or illustrator.

What we have come to define as creative work is oddly narrow and paradoxically unimaginative. 'Creative jobs' are designated with a pretentious wand that positions certain forms of work above others. 'Uncreative' work is deemed to be of lesser value, while 'creatively qualified' members of society are held in high esteem. 'Creatives' are not superior beings. Our cousins/landlords/neighbours are as creative as the rest.

PENPAL YOUR IDOLS

Nobody is too far away (besides the dead). Write to the people you admire. Start a dialogue. Express yourself, be generous, ask for nothing. I wrote to Iggy Pop and he wrote back.

TIRED OF SELF-HELP?

Your self doesn't need to be helped. We are grand as we are, not perpetual works-in-progress.

NEVER MIND THE BULLSHIT

Discover. Engineered. Innovation. Purpose. Engaging. Game-changing. Disruptive... Get out of the hollow-vocab zone. Just because everyone else is saying it, doesn't mean you need to. These terms are overused and abused. We're desensitised to these words anyway.

II

11. DON'T ACCEPT MYTHOLOGY AS REASON

A starving artist does not make better work than one who has been fed.
Overworking is not better than underworking.
There are other modes of time than that which is always urgent.

12. PRO WEIRDNESS
PRO PRIVACY
PRO OFFLINE

13. LIE YOUR WAY IN

If you're convinced you can follow through, nema problema.

14. ALL-URGENT EVERYTHING

When everything is highlighted, nothing is visible.
When everything is loud, nothing is audible.
When everything is urgent, nothing is important.

15. THE JOY OF

Hanging Out
Doing Not Much
Someone Cracking A Joke
Killing Time

These joys only some can afford, or can they?
What would we change to have them?

16. IN THE SAME EXISTENCE WE CAN FIND

The Right to Laziness
The Right to Exhaustion
The Right to Sensuous Slowness
The Right to Naivety and Curiosity
The Right to Unproductivity
The Right to Complain

II

17. MASS APPEAL SCH-MASS APPEAL
Key to marketing success is making sure you don't appeal to everyone. If you try to do everything, you do nothing.

18. SECURITY IS NOT DECADENT
Creativity does not result from removing people's stability. It does not spring forth from strained circumstances, and it does not get more radical the more extreme conditions become. The notion of the starving artist has been romanticised to exhaustion. Be certain that uncertainty is not a given, nor deserved.

19. HUNGRY FOR ANSWERS
When considering offline forms of creativity, does your mind begin blooming with ideas, or does it jump straight to the habit of asking somebody else for answers? Trust yourself.

20. RESISTANCE AS 'AGAINST FROM WITHIN'
You ought to prove to your employer that you're alive.
ELFRIEDE JELINEK

INTERLUDE

PART TWO: RESIST- ANCE

Why are we not rebelling?

With this question, Peter Lang[§] confronts his life in the throes of design education and its intensifying bureaucratic systems. He posited this question in 2018, precisely fifty years after May 1968, that cataclysmic event on Parisian streets. 'We're getting better and better at defining what the threat is, but at the same time we're having a harder and harder time trying to define what the ways of resistance should be.'

Like Lang's straight-up account from the inside, this section of the book shakes the complacency we see at every turn. It wonders how much of that motionlessness is imposed, and how much is self-inflicted. Here is your permission to reconsider that online-everything approach to creativity. Here is your licence to do things differently. Here is your permit to hold onto *creativity* as you want it to be, when the world says it should be data, algorithms, and analytics. This is a call to prioritise enjoyment of life and unreasoned imagination, a challenge to be outside the norm and proud of it. Just because 'everyone's doing it' doesn't mean there is something there. If you prefer otherwise, follow it. To vouch for human connection in-real-life and take an altruistic viewpoint is radical.

Non-conformity can be a lonely place. Fear not, you are not alone. You have comrades who are also doing things differently. Ask the questions nobody's asking. Provoke the possibilities nobody's touching. Give yourself the opportunity to fill in a blank. Undo the inclination to seek external confirmation. You got this.

PETER LANG IS A FORMER PROFESSOR OF ARCHITECTURAL THEORY AND HISTORY AT THE ROYAL INSTITUTE OF ART, STOCKHOLM (2013-2019). §

LIMIT INPUT
Protecting Original Thought

Is it just me, or does everyday life feel like it only gets harder? If we were to map the difficulty experienced doing simple life tasks over time, would its overall curve be on the increase? Sure, now I can get groceries delivered with a single click. And yes, finding that broken part I needed for the washing machine is easier. But overall there is a feeling of friction, a heavy weight dragging at our heels. What is this sensation that seems to make each step more draining than the last, this condition that conspires to siphon off joy?

ENTER THE INFOSPHERE

That whizzing, fascinating, hypnotic whirl of never-ending stimuli that surrounds us 24/7. Accessible night and day via the cherished pal Screen, the infosphere is that beautiful portal to everything you could ever want, wonder, or need. Curious about the current temperature in Beirut? It's there. Feeling bored and want something to do? It's all waiting in your hand. Uncomfortable without reason? Numb that bad boy out. 'It becomes perversely gratifying to use social media as a coping mechanism for the very anxiety it instantiated... Nothing holds our attention better than our own discomfort.'[1]

NEVER NOT OPEN

This immediate all-hours-access to anything and everything has us sinking into debilitation. The more we access it, the more we feel the friction. And this sensation of friction signals to us that something is not quite right. Too much information. Too much stimulation. The relentless pace of the all-giving online world has reached total incompatibility with our human rhythms. Its speed has no limit, the infinite scroll has no end. But we do. We are out of sync and the cracks are showing. Our nervous system cannot handle it. Our brain, in this mushy state, cannot critically understand the world around us. We cannot *criticise*. In the absence of critical thinking, we become vulnerable to over-influence. And we cannot create. Indeed, the slow, organic process of creativity crumbles under the acceleration of the infosphere. The excess of stimuli that keeps us frozen and exhausted is what the precariat worker numbs out to during the day. When without work, or needing a break from overwork, they turn to the reel of images within their handheld device. They unlock the door to influence and one's originality is infiltrated.

TO PARTICIPATE OR WITHDRAW?

Should we leave things be and let it happen, or withdraw completely from a technically-mediated life? That is the default question. Oddly there is only this simplistic binary on offer. Except, we are far past it being that simple. As the online world spins faster and faster, at machinic speed we cannot bear, the typical consideration is whether to 'stay in' or 'get out'. Supposedly there are ways to cope, temporary 'detoxes' that can still take advantage of all the opportunities that the infosphere offers. The other option is that hippy dream, the overall opt-out that takes on a 'back to nature' mindset and abstains absolutely from any interaction with the online world. As you and I both know, neither of these are viable options. Nor are either of them progressions presenting a step forward.

THE THIRD SPACE

Far from nostalgic backwards-harkening ideas, reconsidering what we call 'offline' offers an alternative. An option beyond the binary. A vacant but verdant place, an open expanse alive and ready, a breeding ground for critical thought. Offline is a site waiting to be tilled and turned, fertilised and utilised. What might we use this space for? For provocation. For collaboration. For experimentation. Here we have a space that as quiet and lone – or as vigorously collective as you please. For healing the frictions of life together or realising our dreams in solitude.
Even just knowing about alternatives to the default makes us part of the movement, challenging the present state by thinking and doing things differently. How can we expect this to happen when we're perpetually distracted? The more information we consume, the more our mind and thoughts are influenced. We begin to only react to things, rather than birthing them ourselves. Away from distraction is where originality generates. This is why getting away from that stimuli whirlwind is so essential.

*When you're creating your own shit,
man, even the sky ain't the limit.* MILES DAVIS

VIGILANCE IS KEY

In the infosphere, the potential for new creative thinking becomes muddied with the sheer barrage of inputs received, other people's voices, aesthetics, opinions, and tastes – which itself was probably rehashed and recycled. Hello homogeneity! This is the cult of the same, an environment expert at feeding itself and belching out something that will quickly be re-digested once again.

Writing on the art of self-preservation, Nietzsche insisted that: 'at times when I am deeply sunk in work you will see no books around me: I would guard against letting anyone speak or even think in my vicinity.'[2] This is essential. One needs to cultivate a selectivity about what is let in and how much of it. Besides the question of originality, life online triggers a comparison-reaction that more often results in feelings of inadequacy than boosting of self-belief. Be vigilant.

IS   IT   DIFFICULT   TO   DISCERN
WHAT   IS   YOURS
AND   WHAT   CAME   FROM   ELSEWHERE?

THE NECESSITY OF DEFENCE

Manning the boundaries between offline space and protecting the mind when online both require radical defence. It's a different kind of battle, one that gets easier as the rewards become noticeable. It does not take long to feel the friction start to subside, to feel the mud start to fall away, to sense that the curve of difficulty has become less steep. A levelling out occurs and with it we start to see new ideas arrive. Suddenly different visions appear, visceral opinions emerge, exciting imaginings take flight. This is your new energy – and it is potent as hell. *Offline* may come under siege but it is yours for the taking.

EVERY DAY

It's not in or out, nor off or on. It's an everyday radical activity that tunes into a new space, that cracks open an alternative. This is how to maintain energies – the soft and the hard, the loud and the quiet. Use the offline possibility space to manifest what you know you can do. Or what you want to be able to do. It already lies there. Waiting.

RESTRICT STIMULI.

LIMIT INPUT.

UTILISE OFFLINE.

THE 'JUST BECAUSE' METHOD
Because No Reason is a Reason

In the context of creating, 'Just Because' is electric thinking. It is a method, a practice, and a rationale. I am handing it over to you with full permission to say it's yours. Go forth with it. Use it to put your thought, work, creativity, and way of life into a different frame.

Just Because defies all aspects of the 'creativity-as-product' machine. It stands in opposition to the traditional consumer-seller exchange that has ossified. Just Because is an action with no commercial motive (not to be confused with no *apparent* commercial motive). Just Because acknowledges that everything is marketing, then forgets everything it knew marketing to be. Just Because utterly embraces the idea that no reason is a reason. It is the willingness for surprise.

DOING THINGS

JUST BECAUSE.

Just Because is making because you had an idea and you like it and so does everyone else. Just Because it would be fun to do. Just Because isn't based on data. It wasn't suggested by algorithms and it wasn't in a report from a trend forecaster. Just Because is an expression of the moment, an impulse, a desire to make something happen because it feels right. Just Because is doing what's urgent, relevant, intriguing – or none of these at all. Just Because is responsive and yet not resting on a speculative future. It is what feels exciting *today*.

True art is always there where no one is waiting for it...
Art does not come and lie in the beds we make for it.
It slips away as soon as its name is uttered;
it likes to preserve its incognito.
Its best moments are when it forgets its very name.

JEAN DUBUFFET

Just Because is the forgetting of its name, the nature of itself, that creativity as work needs. Creative expression that's not for sale. A joy to make, a joy to witness, a joy to receive. It is against the financialisation of everything. It is for breaking through by breaking forth. It is unlearning what has been learnt, loosening up what has fossilised. Just Because exposes the dull structures that lie beneath. It questions the rigid rules that separate the 'legitimate' from the 'illegitimate'. It is an answer to the question of 'why?' that cannot be handled. Within our normal lives, the idea of anything existing 'without reason' has become offensive. *'What's the purpose? What's the return? What's the point? Just, why?'* Creation that does not 'perform', optimise, grow, profit, or return with revenue, is pointless.

POINTLESS IS POINTED

The pointless has never been so pointed. It embodies all the everyday luxuries we long for and all we lament as missing. Curiosity, play, experiment, the Zen wisdom of not knowing. The pointless is what's most pertinent. To answer 'why?' with Just Because is to push back against the demolition of everyday surrealism. This is a kind of wonder that whisks you away from reality like a split in the system. It finds a crack and hammers at it with glee, accidentally revealing more than it sought to. Something that takes you away and brings you to a new place, then drops you right back where you were with a change you can and can't put your finger on. It is sensational to experience something that didn't 'have a reason' to be there but somehow is. A moment broken open with something that didn't exist a second ago. The rare experience of a separation from expectation. The pointless might just be the remedy to re-enchant the disenchanted.

You are waiting to cross the street, standing there paused until the red man turns green. The mind ticks over with what's to be done, when suddenly somebody from behind puts their hands over your eyes and says: 'Guess who?' You're shocked, but the voice is one you know. You're not sure how. Family? Friend? Who? No one is jumping to mind. Unfrozen, you turn around to see none other than Bill Murray standing there with a grand smirk. Speechless, you stare as he softly says 'No one will ever believe you' and walks away.

Surreal to the point of being unbelievable, variations on this occurrence have surrounded Murray for a decade. When he wasn't covering the eyes of a pedestrian, he was helping himself to popcorn from the neighbouring cinema-watcher, or joining a garden party he heard next door, uninvited. All closed with that amazing line. At first it was unclear whether the tales were an urban legend gone wild or something Murray actually did. There are countless anecdotes online of people sharing their encounters, all across the United States. Whenever asked directly, he skilfully dances to keep the wonder alive. 'I've heard about that from a lot of people... by God, it sounds crazy doesn't it? Just so crazy and unlikely and unusual?' This is the epitome of Just Because.

Too much is misunderstood as pointless. What do you get from reading fiction as best-seller lists become full of non-fiction?[§] Maybe you cannot articulate it exactly, but you cannot say that it is pointless. The so-called pointless is where we unhinge the context of expectation, which explodes the patterns that hold our cynicism and narrow our imaginative potential. It's exactly what is needed for a radical breakout. Breaking the hypnosis of busy-but-bored life. It's that challenge, that prank, that unexplainable strangeness. It's the break*through*. What distinguishes a regular city wall from one scrawled with a surprise statement, or a simple newspaper versus a xeroxed monochrome zine, is the ripping apart of old forms and structures to create new perceptions which renew and refresh life itself.

Obedience to language, image, and behaviour must continually be challenged if we are to stay 'alive.'[‡1]

A CRACK IN STAGNANT 'CREATIVITY'

Just Because as a vehicle drives head-first into all that we feel has made 'creativity' sad and stagnant. The data, the reason, the rules, the greed, and the homogeneity – everything that blocks any potential fun or revelation. Doing things Just Because allows imagination, selflessness, and surprise to erupt. They promote the weird over the safe.

Imagine reasoning decisions by saying, let's do it...

... just because it feels right.
... just because it would be fun.
... just because it's weird!
... just because I'm curious what would happen.
... just because I'd like to see that.
... just because we want to.

BECAUSE   NO   REASON
IS   A   REASON

Just Because breaks through banality and hits you like a brick. Just Because breeds enthusiasm. Just Because retains the lust for what you do, resists the deceleration of 'typical processes', and trusts that your vision is more to the moment than an algorithm's suggestion. It is the disdain for everything having become so fucking boring. It is that scathing *meaningful by being meaningless* that we so desperately need. It's the follow-up to surrealism that never happened. An investigation into absurdity. *How weird can you go?* A moment that transfixes, sweeps away, and returns in a totally new way. As though nothing changed. Except everything. Ushering in anything unasked for, Just Because is a life accentuated.

Just Because is permission to create at the most explosive level. This could be the method that keeps us enriched, alive, and challenging – or simply an enjoyment of how it feels to find the reasonless. In a time where everything needs reason to exist, defiance is extreme. Allowing ambiguity is the height of tolerance in an intolerant world Asking for absurdity displeases the order. Though, if the 'unnecessary' can already be seen as decadent, does that make Just Because luxurious, a deluxe form of creation? In the midst of our arid 'work environments', is unreasoned and extreme creativity the *crème de la crème* of what can be brought to life?

THE POINTLESS POINTING TO OUR LIVES

People loved the apparition of guerrilla knitting. To wander a street you had wandered a million times and discover a tree now hugged in psychedelic craft. The cracking of a smile. 'When did that happen? Who put that there? Why?' A heartfelt sensation of wonder. Followed freakishly by the embodied discomfort of not knowing and an inability to get the answer. This is a reflection of our lives – a known deficiency in delight and noticeable distress at a 'why?' that will always remain unanswerable.

DESIRE & DISTRACTION
Socialising as an Antidote to Consumerism

The pull of consumerism is everywhere. We are bombarded with messages seducing us to spend, then leaving us with the notion that possessing things confirms our success, confirms that we are doing okay, and confirms a happiness that we can hold.

In this piece we consider, what if we instead used consumerism as an agent of change? Redirected the disdain and discomfort into a momentum to get off the couch and out into the world. To go offline and get together face-to-face – where simply socialising could be not just resistance, but the site of reaction. Of radical reimagining. An IRL jamming of new strategies, ideas, and dreams.

...the whole selfie, internet narcissism trip – they're training people to stay inside.[1]   GENESIS BREYER P-ORRIDGE

RECLAIMING OUR DESIRES

Think about it. When we are physically together, our interactions relieve the emotional tensions advertisers play on. Our desires are reclaimed. Capital and greed prey on desire. They want it all to themselves. When our phones and computers became direct channels for us to be marketed to, it blurred the lines between life, connection, and communication, with that of capital-at-large. Now, the desire for a phone – that is in fact not a desire for the phone itself but the very human wish to be able to call your mother when you are travelling, or do your banking, or organise your shifts, or record an interview for research – becomes indistinguishable from a consumerist desire. And that begs the question: is the phone itself the problem? Where is the exit from this muddle of distraction? We are being moved away from our desire to get together and towards an increasingly individualised existence. This is the distraction that is diverting our innate, instinctual pull to one another. Our libidos are dampened. Our driving lust for life and for meeting physically is being dulled (this is and isn't about sexual encounters). We can call it a loss of erotic want for people over goods. A drive to have elegant possessions over being receptive to the world.

Pleasure is a cultural weapon. Use it wisely.
GENESIS P-ORRIDGE

WHERE   IS   YOUR   LIBIDO?
REDIRECT   YOUR   WANTS.

Can you bring consciousness to your desire and redirect it? Could we shift our wants instead towards alternatives? Could we combat pervasive negative advertising by counter-branding it as post-capitalism?

ANTI VS. POST

Anti-Capitalist is passé. No Logo doesn't work. We need to think beyond and we need to dream of next. Clearly, hating Starbucks and classing it as basic does nothing. As Mark Fisher reminded us: 'Nothing runs better on MTV than a protest against MTV.' Post a pic of your riot and see how many likes you get. What if we instead considered the success of the 'the third place' that Starbucks proposes – a meeting place that is neither work nor home – as a sign that getting together IRL has potency and is desired. There is still something in that idea. An offline space away from the boundless intensification of life (online), free from the distractions of unimportant shit, with a distance from the overstimulation of underwhelming drivel. 'Good conversation is euphoric. It builds and builds.'[+2] What do we desire? Are we longing for coffee or connection?

Distraction is a corporate neutralising agent.
Distraction and isolation.
Subvert these control mechanisms.[+3]   V. VALE

OFFLINE IS NOT NOSTALGIC

Reemphasising the desire for in-person socialising can act as a counter-libido to consumerism. The desire for IRL is not reminiscent of the past. It is opening a future. It projects an alternate real-life than the one we feel is inevitable. The Precarious Workers Brigade suggests how we might transform workplaces and social gatherings into places to rejig desire. 'We make support structures and shared spaces to re-think how our desires, which are currently directed into individualised, competitive, hierarchic modes of being, can instead be oriented toward other forms of common culture.'[+4]

Far from being a stereotypical attack on consumerism, this antidote is post-capitalism in action. It's what happens *after* that boring sense of a commodified-everything. It's an antidote to a life confused about what's important and what is necessity. In each other's company we can forget what seemed so *essential* moments before. Those tensions melt away. I like this because it is a desirable future that can start immediately. An easily-imagined change in how we exacerbate ugly feelings and escape relentless distraction. It's a clever commitment to revolution that rides our nature as creatures of desire. And we can all be part of its vanguard.

People do not know what they want
until they are presented with it.
Nobody knows what they desire.[+5]   KODWO ESHUN

IMPOSTER   NON-SYNDROME
Being Where They Don't Want Us

'Imposter Syndrome' is a problematic piece of jargon. It flaunts itself as a medical term (it's not) that encourages people to blame themselves for structural unfairness. Feeling out of place at work doesn't mean you have a psychological shortcoming – it means that the environment is falling short.

We suffer the 'symptoms' of feeling like an imposter. We read about how to 'cure' our anxieties and attain confidence. But popular media and self-help trash have completely misunderstood this sense of not belonging, this malaise about being undeserving of one's position. This feeling emerges from a systemic bias, not an individual disease. It is systematic inequalities that cause us, and particularly those from minority, working class, or disadvantaged backgrounds, to feel like imposters. Nathalie Olah explains:

What far-reaching and harmful message are we sending out when we paint the natural reaction of working-class and marginalised people as evidence of some kind of 'syndrome'?

Some will say it's only a word, not a medical diagnosis, but it represents an attempt to individualise a structural issue, and to place the burden of responsibility at the door of the undervalued or excluded. This only adds to the list of things that working-class and marginalised people already have to contend with on a daily basis...

...It's important for all of us to remain vigilant to the many ways in which [internalising the structural shame imposed by the corporate workplace] dehumanises us and strips us of our identity.[‡1]

ACKNOWLEDGING TRIUMPH

To my fellow imposters,

For starters, congratulations for making it to the inside. If you're experiencing a sense of imposterdom, that means you are doing something radical rather than wrong. And that is precisely the point!

You are somewhere you are 'not supposed to be' – and that is a prime position for change and influence.

Be what's causing chaos in your field.   JOHN WATERS

The good thing about people who are corporate is that they're stupid. So they can be touching something that's precious or radical or special, and they miss the point completely.   GENESIS P-ORRIDGE

CHAOS AS YOU DEFINE IT

Causing chaos from the inside doesn't have to mean loud and vicious. It can be quiet and subtle. Gradual rather than aggressive. Radical qualities considered 'ineffective' and 'too feminine' to the masculine-skew of workplaces today. Most imposter advice revolves around 'increasing your confidence', which translates to mimicking the types of displays valued as 'strong communication and leadership styles' in our societies. This typically means loud voices, big body language, and other hyper-masculine ideals of what constitutes a leader. The leader, we are told, needs to have a 'visible presence' and possess advanced debating abilities – all behaviours taught in private schools, universities, and upper and middle-class spaces. Being a radical insider doesn't mean playing along. It can mean flipping the script entirely.

IMPOSTERS MOVE THINGS FORWARD

Imposters have always been the ones pushing culture forward. Transgressive creations rarely come from the minds of the comfortable and welcome.

IMPOSTORDOM AS *TRIUMPH* AND *POTENTIAL* RATHER THAN DEFICIENCY

Hold onto the knowledge that this 'syndrome' of being out of your depth is a harmful message. We do not have a disorder. These feelings are natural reactions to the biases we face on a daily basis. This pseudo-syndrome is a structural issue, not an individual problem. It's not an ailment 'in our minds' and it's not our job to remove the sense of it. What we can do now is begin the work of reframing.

IMPOSTERS AS SUCCESSFUL INFILTRATORS

Take a new stance on sensations of imposterdom. When outsiders become insiders, the necessary disturbance happens. The radical creativity and activity can begin. Keep on imposting.

PRECIOUS   KILLS
Too Much Consideration Becomes Doubt

Surrounded by more information, thoughts, distractions, and entertainment than we can keep up with, we are constantly exposed to the amazing things being accomplished by amazing people. Everybody is making the most of their moment and maxing out their capabilities. It is intimidating. We find ourselves using each other as a measuring stick, an involuntary reaction to the all-pervasive concept of the 'personal brand'. What's yours and how are you presenting yourself to the world? Remember, it is designable. You have control so be sure you're making all the *right* decisions. Strategy and scrutiny are key.

If all one's attempts and actions are brought before a jury, who would dare experiment and play? If there were any situation to destroy ideas and the wonderful freedom that creativity allows, it is this one. There is nothing thrilling about self-surveillance, let alone the scrutiny of online eyes. But let's stick with the pressure we inflict upon ourselves. No doubt this is a result of the sensation that *everything must count. I must be brilliant.* That overwhelming 'success' we bear witness to from peers – both known and unknown – whips our inner critic into the cruellest of masters.

When everything you do becomes a question of 'is it post-worthy or not?', the stakes become too high. Your explosive ideas and creative actions never see the light of day. Instead, the world simmers down, becoming an environment of relentless self-censorship. We are under the impression that perfection exists. Anything less than flawless should not be considered.[§] Eventually nothing makes the grade, and we enter that sad weird zone where nothing happens because nothing is good enough. Everything gets risk-managed to ruins. Finally, one day, creativity just calcifies. Frozen in pursuit of perfection.

[§] THE OPTIMISATION OF CREATIVITY HAS SURELY AFFECTED OUR PERCEPTION OF A 'RIGHT' OR 'WRONG' OPTION EXISTING. YOUR WRITING CAN BE SEO-IFIED TO GET MORE CLICKS AND WHICH FILTER YOU CHOOSE CAN DETERMINE HOW SUCCESSFUL THE POST IS. THE WORKPLACE AMPS UP THE DELUSION. WHEN YOUR CREATIVITY FALLS INTO THIS UNDENIABLE JUDGEMENT SYSTEM, EFFICACY RULES. NOW THERE IS A CREATIVITY THAT IS SUPERIOR. AND WE ARE LEFT BELIEVING THERE IS A BEST.

WHAT ARE WE WAITING FOR?

We are bursting with ideas. But how many of them come to light? We *hum* and we *ha*, we criticise ourselves before we even begin. Too much consideration causes doubt. That's how the mean voice creeps in. It's a matter of sprinting forth and outrunning the possibility of cutting ourselves off. Retain confidence in the experiment. Refuse to let the spirit hollow. Make. Fast.

They say 'don't let perfect be the enemy of good'. How about:

IDEAS ARE LIKE FOOD.
USE THEM WHILE THEY'RE FRESH
– OR THEY ROT.

PRECIOUS KILLS

Don't be precious! Make, throw, try, freak out – what have we got to lose? Activity, being responsive, and making all those heady ideas come to life beats sitting on them, deliberating and having them slowly peter out. Quick isn't dirty. You know the traps that halt the energy and potency of ideas. Don't get caught in some loop debating the details. Don't get stuck seeking perfection. You'll never find it.

TOO MUCH CONSIDERATION BECOMES DOUBT

Drive yourself into fearlessness. It's a collective emancipatory project. Encourage those around you. Assure them that getting it right is a fallacy and freezing is a risk of thinking otherwise. Put your blinders on, avoid comparing, and make what you want – not what any supposed data or platform pressure suggests.

AIM   LOWER
The   Realities   of   Time   Perception

Any task you're planning to complete will always take longer than expected. That's a fact. Did a rush of relief flow down your shoulders after reading that? It turns out that our daily frustration of *I've only accomplished half of what I wanted to do today* is a common human phenomenon. Even if we account for a task to overrun and add a time buffer, it will overrun that too. Project Managers around the world can breathe a little easier; it is not your fault that projects often extend far beyond their anticipated length. Cognitive scientist Douglas Hofstadter researched and identified this issue in the 1950s, a phenomenon that has since come to be known as 'Hofstadter's Law'.

It always takes longer than you expect, even when you take into account Hofstadter's law.[‡1]   HOFSTADTER

CHRONIC UNDERESTIMATION

Underestimating is not new. Even before our present day, with its army of devices for distraction and procrastination, we would underestimate the time needed for the task at hand. And chronically so. All scales of activity were susceptible to this miscalculation, from small chores like writing a letter to bigger feats like building the Sydney Opera House, which opened a decade later than scheduled. Yet somehow this information still feels new. Our unrealistic vision of what is achievable in a day runs counter to popular productivity and time-management narratives. The mantra here is to achieve total efficiency, to accomplish the maximum in the minimum amount of time. These are hot topics that attract eyeballs to websites, drive pupils to advice gurus, and send books to the top of bestseller lists. At a time when everyone laments how little hours there are in a day, time management tips have never been such a big business.

Intuitively, it feels sensible to work out in detail what your projects involve, to break them into chunks and estimate how long each part will take.
But the problem with unforeseen delays is you can't foresee them.[2]

OLIVER BURKEMAN

One industry that has long recognised Hofstadter's Law is computer programming and software engineering. Hofstadter first discussed the law in his Pulitzer Prize-winning *Gödel, Escher, Bach: An Eternal Golden Braid*, a book that gained popularity among American programmers. The fact that tasks take longer than we calculate has become something of an inside joke in the industry. 'The first 90 percent of the code accounts for the first 90 percent of the development time. The remaining 10 percent of the code accounts for the other 90 percent of the development time.'[3]

WHAT'S THE PLAN?

Does this mean that planning is a fallacy we are unable to acknowledge? We know things take longer than expected – but somehow we seem to repeatedly forget it. What appears to be short-term memory loss is really a form of wishful thinking, a bias towards believing otherwise. These biases can be sorted into three categories:

1. Optimism Bias
    When people predict the time a task will take, they base their estimations on the steps required but fail to allow for anything to go wrong. This bias could also be known as *Best Case Scenario*.

2. Superiority Bias
    People overrate their own positive qualities[4] and underrate their negative ones when compared with others. It sounds like: 'This would take someone else three hours, but I'll only need two'.

3. Beneffectance Bias
    People perceive themselves as selectively accountable for all the factors that may impact the desired outcome. It sounds like: 'This took longer than expected last week but only because that thing came up. Today I have full control, so it should take just 20 minutes'.

WHAT TO DO?

Aim lower. That's right. Give yourself a break! Allow for a check-in on what is realistically achievable in the time given. Trust your intuition. We can sense when that to-do list is overly ambitious and only setting ourselves up to fall short. Equally important is limiting your exposure to productivity articles and feeds that promote a distorted view of what's possible, and of the levels of other people's creative outputs.

See if you're overcommitting. Instead of juggling many tasks, try focusing on one thing at a time. Address where time pressures are being applied from and if unrealistic deadlines are being imposed on you. Flagging that project schedule as overly optimistic or even naïve can be a signifier of wisdom that everyone was waiting for, but no one was saying.

GETTING REAL ABOUT TIME
IS NOT *SLACKER*,

IT'S REALITY.

IT'S SAYING WHAT NO ONE ELSE
IS SAYING.

PLAN SCHLAN

How about we avoid planning altogether? Take an ad-hoc approach and adjust course as you go along.[‡5] Skip ready and aim, go straight to fire. See what happens. What will become apparent is real feedback. Not guesstimated results, not algorithmic predictions, but a real ability to make to the moment, to respond to the situation, to give exactly what is needed.

Or simply tone down the level of detail and get comfortable with the time required. Refreshingly frank, writer and theorist Eliezer Yudkowsky writes:

...The unlikely trick is to plan in less detail: avoid considering the specifics and simply ask yourself how long it's taken to do roughly similar things before. You'll get back an answer that sounds hideously long, and clearly reflects no understanding of the special reasons why this task will take less time. This answer is true. Deal with it.[‡6]

SLOW IS COUNTER-CULTURAL

Engaging in the process of slowing down is counter-cultural, which is why this all sounds so foreign. 'Slow movements' are talked about, but the word slow still gets associated with lag, with being behind, with laziness. In actuality, acknowledging that things take longer than we expect and that it is okay to take that time is anything but lazy. It is 100% *ahead*.

Can we invent a new language for slow? It starts with extracting ourselves from the tangle of unrealistic time pressures we have become caught up in. It begins by recalibrating our life and our tasks to a more realistic rhythm. Give yourself time to absorb ideas, to connect the dots, to flow, adjust, and adapt. This is a more humane time. A time proportioned to what's realistic. A time proportioned to our capacity. A time proportioned to our happiness. Otherwise, what's the point?

Arrrrrrrrrrrrgh arrrrrrgh arrrgghhhh! More more more! We need to do more! And this sort of hyperventilating, hyperactive reaction to late capitalism's ills. Don't mimic the system's rhythm of instantaneous reactions and snap decisions. Get off the treadmill. If we let ourselves be in this state of panic, we won't be able to cope; people are already burning out and retreating into themselves, internalising and feeding off individualised distractions as a coping mechanism.[‡7]

NADIA IDLE

INTERLUDE
INTERLUDE
INTERLUDE
INTERLUDE
INTERLUDE
INTERLUDE
INTERLUDE
INTERLUDE

1. COUNTERPRODUCTIVE

Why are we so terrified of this word? What's so scary about being idle?

2. GIMME DANGER

Bring on discomfort. Ask for it. Seek it out. Changing and challenging
can hurt before what's next arrives. 'Social change isn't painless' said
Jodi Dean. Goodbye individualist rhetorics of self-care. Put yourself
second. We can be for meaningful hedonism as we are for chafing
one's self in life to see what happens.

3. PRO NON-FORMAL TRAINING

When they are giving out master's degrees in 'Disruption', it's time to
acknowledge that formal training is not an indication of capability.

4. COULDN'T HAVE SAID IT BETTER

*What you don't necessarily realise when you start
selling your time by the hour is that what you're
really selling is your life.* BARBARA EHRENREICH

5. 'BEST PRACTICE' GUIDES ARE CLICK-MAGNETS

If your boss reads 'Ten Ways to Enhance Engagement' clickbait in the
morning and brings it as a great new idea to a meeting in the afternoon
– you're not alone.

III

6. A NEW FORM OF WORKING-FOR-FREE: ARE YOU THE (UNPAID) STAR?

Special mention to the latest employer cost-saving trick, using employees in marketing campaigns. If your employer is trying the trend of getting their workforce to star in campaigns, know that this should not go unpaid. Whether you're asked to give a quote and photo for social media content, voice a podcast ad, or be filmed for a TV spot, this is labour that requires remuneration. And it certainly is not remunerated with the 'specialness of being one of the few chosen to face the brand.'

7. LEADER OR MANAGER?

The difference between leadership and management is that leadership is human and management is structural. The primal job of leadership is emotional. A leader's fundamental role is to prime a good feeling in the people they lead, to create emotional resonance in the group. This creates a reservoir of respect that frees up the best in people. Anybody can be a leader and it is likely, possible, but not ideal, that your boss may not be your leader.

8. MIND YOUR TIME

Your time is your most valuable asset. Your time = Your life. Consider all those times when you've said, 'If only I had an extra 20 minutes in the day...' Meditation! Painting! Running! [INSERT LONGED-FOR ACTIVITY HERE]! Don't give that away.

9. BACK OFF

I'm overloaded with content. Your 'Skip This In 5... 4...' ads make me think you're lame and annoying. I'd be far more likely to enjoy my morning coffee if you didn't ask me to get the app every time I visit the page. Audience satisfaction is at an all-time low. Go figure. Wake up from the confusion that these online assaults do magic for a brand. Do not keep digitally bombarding me with things that cost you a fortune and make me dislike you.

10. IMPORTANT IS DIFFERENT TO URGENT

Determine what's what. Know the difference.

III
INTERLUDE
INTERLUDE
INTERLUDE
INTERLUDE
INTERLUDE
INTERLUDE
INTERLUDE

CONSCIOUSNESS — RAISING
Your Activism Starts Now

Consciousness-raising is a form of activism. It is the drawing of attention to a condition or cause by getting together to talk about it. In sharing experiences, we learn that our problems are not necessarily personal but are caused by broader structures. We discover that we're all experiencing the same thing. Consciousness-raising was a key tool utilised by historical social movements, from the feminist movement of the 1970s to later strands of gay liberation and black power. In 1967, member of New York Radical Women Anne Forer described the early identification of the tool's power:

In the Old Left, they used to say that the workers don't know they're oppressed, so we have to raise their consciousness... One night at a meeting I said, 'Would everybody please give me an example from their own life on how they experience oppression as a woman? I need to hear it to raise my own consciousness.[1]

There is no single method for consciousness-raising. However, small group discussion is extremely effective at breaking down the isolation from one another that makes us misunderstand many of our problems as personal, resulting from the personality conflicts of individuals rather than systemic forms of oppression.

HELLO PRECARITY

Every phase of capitalism has a dominant affect, and that affect is always a public secret.[2] Something we all know but nobody talks about. A mechanism of control. The dominant affect and public secret of our phase is anxiety.

All forms of intensity, self-expression, emotional connection, immediacy, and enjoyment are now laced with anxiety. It has become the linchpin of subordination.[3]

INSTITUTE FOR PRECARIOUS CONSCIOUSNESS

P124

We are surveilled 24/7, both from 'above' and from one another. Life is a constant performance of portrayed success (lookin' at you social media, lookin' at you conversations with friends, lookin' at you parental advice), from what you're eating to what you're working on. And since everyone is disposable if you don't perform accordingly you risk being 'delinked'. Delinking can mean being cut off socially, for instance, think of how many people report wanting to leave Facebook but stay for the events and birthday notifications. It can also mean not getting work or being unable to access bureaucratic systems. No wonder we're all anxious! It is (no) public secret that life is a fierce competition and we need to be always-on. The dominant affect[§] of our anxiety is precarity. Precarity is the word for that absence of security in our lives that controls us by treating us as disposable.

NO LONGER A PUBLIC SECRET

Strategies against precarity can only emerge if it's no longer a public secret. That's why consciousness-raising is so effective. Talking about our situation and feelings out loud, with others, creates the potential for responses to emerge. We discover overlaps in our lives and find these overlaps are caused by the structures we're living in. We learn that our discomforts are imposed from the outside and not personal downfalls.[§§]

'I'm definitely working more hours than I'm billing them for.'

'When I packed up my desk to leave on time yesterday, my boss said "working half days now?"'

'I felt like if I negotiated too hard, they might retract the offer all together.' ANECDOTES RECORDED ON THE INSIDE

AFFECT: EMOTION, BODILY DISPOSITION, WAY OF RELATING [§]

'THE TRUTH IS OF COURSE STRUCTURAL, AND THE PERPETUATION OF ANXIETY IS PART [§§]
AND PARCEL OF THE SYSTEM AND HOW IT OPERATES. IF YOU ARE IN A PRECARIOUS
JOB AND HOUSING SITUATION LIKE MANY PEOPLE ARE, YOU WILL HAVE LESS MENTAL
SPACE FOR POLITICAL ACTION, AND WILL OFTEN BE WAY TOO EXHAUSTED AND
STRESSED OUT TO GO TO THAT CAMPAIGN MEETING ON HOW TO SAVE THIS OR THAT
OR FIGHT YET ANOTHER FIRE.' - NADIA IDLE

Consciousness-raising is crucial in showing us how common thoughts like these are. Getting together offline is powerful. We need this face-to-face sharing of experiences to find our commonalities. One key commonality is the experience of stress. We are told that stress is an individual psychological problem. It is up to us to fix ourselves. This is incorrect as it places all responsibility on the individual, rather than the conditions and structures that are causing it. Go to yoga! Start meditating! Overwhelmed by your job? Get better organised! Productivity problems? Read a book on time management! These ideas are dangerous, especially when experienced alone. Isolation hides the flaws in these concepts.

GETTING   CONSCIOUS
ON   WORK   TIME

Your activism can start right here, right now. Hijack your work lunch with the question 'How do you feel at the end of a day's work?'. Next time you're having beers with friends ask 'Are you ever unobserved?' or 'How does telling people what you do for money make you feel?'. If these concepts are compelling to you, why not organise a consciousness-raising session with friends, friends of friends, neighbours – whomever! You don't have to know everyone. Here are some questions to get you started:

- How much of your time do you spend thinking about work?
- Does your work affect your home life?
- Have you ever felt burnt out?
- How does your workplace recognise, treat, or handle exhaustion?
- What do you do to manage your reputation?
- Do you know what will be paying your bills in six months' time?
- What would happen if you went AWOL for a day?
- What parts of yourself are unwelcome in the market?
- Who do you compete with?
- Who do you care for? Who cares for you?
- Do you feel pressure around self-development?
- How much sleep do you get?

...We may have more formally called it 'Consciousness-Raising', but in essence we were telling each other stories to reclaim our lives and our humanity... We didn't have to all tell the same story in order to resonate with each other.

LORETTA. J. ROSS

NOT RANTING, NOT THERAPY

Our public secret is protected by a culture of silence. In order to overthrow it, we need to take back the truth and our reality – shift it from the system back to the speaker. By exercising our voices together, we can change the way we see things. The perspective shifts, moving from the system's viewpoint to our own. Our own vision and desires. We break down the isolated existences that maintain power structures. It's not about bashing your boss, nor is it therapy (although the result may feel therapeutic).

SELF-DISCLOSURE
AS A MEANS OF
SELF-EMANCIPATION

THINK ABOUT IT

If we all know how much each other is earning, then the employer loses the power from their salary oppression mechanisms. This doesn't mean to say you have to make everything private public, but by increasing our vulnerability and revealing that we are experiencing pains or not happy all of the time, we break the silence that fortifies the situation. 'Take as much space as you can. And when you come up against obstacles in trying to throw the best party, make it visible how and why you weren't allowed to.'[+4]
If we want to talk everyday resistance and empowerment, this is it.

We believe that revolutionary strategy must always be based on collective discussions on the experience of life.

PLAN-C MOVEMENT

LONG LIVE OFFLINE INTERACTION

This has to happen together. IRL is powerful, virtual can do too. Collectively overcoming the alienating individualism of online culture. Here is our ability to reveal the structures that exist around us and confirm that we are part of something bigger. We are members of a whole, we are not alone, and we are strategising together.

CONTEMPLATION:
WHY DOES 'CONSCIOUSNESS' SOUND STALE?

When I first learnt of consciousness-raising as a practice, the word 'consciousness' was off-putting. It called to mind corporate wellbeing set-ups that bring meditation into the workplace, or trends of psychedelics' revival. There was a staleness and corporate feel to it that nearly made me dismiss it before I had even learnt what it was. It had the same decayed quality, which has stripped words like 'sustainability', 'innovation', and even 'activism' of any real impact. Crossing the following passage helped me understand that reaction and how it came to be:

Language, typically the most essential method by which we articulate our affective life, can be a most insidious means of our own oppression if co-opted by those who would exploit us.

There is a reason why re-emergent words and phrases like 'solidarity', 'class consciousness', 'mass movement', 'organize', and 'collective struggle' sound old-fashioned and in need of a good dusting-off. They didn't simply fall out of vogue; they were aggressively obsolesced in our everyday lives by a variety of interests— employers, corporations hungrily eyeing public assets—determined to alienate us from each other in the interest of marketising our souls for their own benefit.[+5]

Let's not fall into the delusion, dismissing these words as outdated or irrelevant. There is a reason why, when creative work found calling people customers or consumers too honest, we switched to 'community'. And now community has got that icky-feel too.

ADHOCISM
A   Case   for   the   Anti-Plan

Ad-hoc has got a bad rap. Negative connotations have been attached to it over time to the point where it has morphed into a workplace insult synonymous with poor planning, reactionary measures, irritating and avoidable situations, and general amateurism. These associations have diverged far from its original meaning. In the 1970s, when the term 'adhocism' was coined, the definition was:

Adhocism is the art of living and doing things ad-hoc — tackling problems at once, using materials at hand, rather than waiting for the perfect moment or 'proper' approach.[1]

Sounds like us, right?

When you strip it back further to the Latin phrase *Ad Hoc*, it literally means 'for this' or 'for this situation'. What an injustice we are doing these two little words by attaching them to inadequacy when, in fact, to be ad-hoc means the total opposite. It means to be responsive and specific. It means to make what is *bespoke*. It calls for instinct and improvisation.

Adhocism urges us to pay less attention to the rulebook and more to reality. It lets us address what is actually unfolding around us. It utilises adaptation, common sense, and trust in ourselves to know what is needed right now. It bypasses the delays typical of bureaucratic and hierarchical organisations, and this makes ad-hoc creation a method of radicality. Ad-hoc undermines approved procedures and expected processes. Ad-hoc loves and discards reason.

To be responsive, to act spontaneously, to meet a particular end, to do things that fall outside the paradigm of pre-strategised outcome and clear objectives *is* creativity! It is creativity in its most unadulterated and humane form. Free from official planning and free from rules, ad-hoc creation is more intuitive, truthful, and alive than the outputs of the traditional process.

AD-HOC AS A WAY OF WORK

Creating with immediacy and spontaneity frees one up to do what fits and makes sense to the situation, *right now*. By thinking on the spot and avoiding potential over-consideration, we also dodge the doubt that typically creep in when given time. The immediacy of ad-hoc frees us and our making from becoming too reserved, from hedging our bets and getting overly cautious. Without these fears we reach a rare experience of freedom. A place to transcend patterns, conventions, and rule-governed behaviour.

It is a method that speaks to us at a primal level. We are naturally inventive and improvisation is hardwired into us, inextricable to the simple pursuit of survival. Sociologist Richard Sennett connects ad-hoc creation to our post-industrial selves. At a time when most of us create very little and derive our primary sense of self from what we consume, we find ourselves increasingly alienated from a source of true meaning – that of skilful making.[+2] Ad-hoc revives the impulse to *make* and the consequential impact that comes with it.

Ad-hoc is an undeveloped force, one that runs against the way we typically approach almost every activity, from design and urban development to cooking or partying. Common in today's working environments are development processes, feedback processes, approval processes – all forms of red tape that cause demotivation, dilution, and deceleration. Don't get caught in some loop, seeking some imagined perfection. You'll never find it.

A METHOD FOR FRESHNESS

Ideas do not have the chance to become stale when acted upon promptly. Bringing them to life quickly keeps the momentum that makes things relevant. Hierarchical organisations of commercial creativity are indifferent to the nature of the creative process. Over time, they have morphed further and further into factories of tired, tortured ideas. Ideas stalled and 'streamlined' along the production line, shoved into a standard mould that is a shadow of its original self (the thing you fought to put in) – a shadow that is late to the party.

Ad-hoc creations guarantee freshness and ad-hoc approaches can experience real feedback. Not 'predictions' generated by robbed data or programmed algorithms. No, these are live responses, from alive people, to alive action that takes place in front of them. The insights that can be gathered with ad-hoc actions show it is more than an exercise in lateral thinking, it is a strategic tool. Jane Fulton Suri explains in her book *Thoughtless Acts* (her term for our instinctual ad-hoc improvisations) that when a person is triggered to make a change in their environment, it signifies a functional deficiency. For example, when a table is wobbly, we instantly look for an impromptu wedge to stabilise it. Or when a traffic island becomes an illegal trash-disposal, local residents transform it into a pétanque court. During times of political revolution, we see new, unprecedented forms of self-protection being invented, like umbrellas, masks, or strange tape on faces to prevent facial recognition. These solutions show us that ad-hoc is a natural research tool.[‡3] We are in our primal ad-hoc habitat when we need to find an answer.

An adhocracy is... any form of organisation that cuts across normal bureaucratic lines to capture opportunities, solve problems, and get results.[‡4]

BECOME AN ADHOCRACY

As Waterman's definition above suggests, the introduction of adhocism as a style of organisation in the 90s put it in line to be taken seriously. This was a way of running a business that did not compromise results, whatever those results may be.

Creative agencies attempt to understand the zeitgeist with methods that lack momentum. The absence of this energy highlights a different urgency – a financial one. While efficiency and productivity have no place in creative freedom, here they are given all the importance. Perhaps your ways of working, whether personal or creativity-as-work, have been conditioned by these values. When we practice adhocism, we are quickly made aware that there are no rules. This is why we are here. To question everything. To be reminded that we can unlearn things we didn't ask to be taught. We can deconstruct adopted habits and tendencies that lean towards invisible directives. Go outside these automatic behaviours, using ad-hoc as a vehicle.

FRET LESS.

DO MORE.

FINAL ENCOURAGEMENT
From a conversation with legendary punk publisher and extreme anthropologist V. Vale:

Do you believe in working ad-hoc?

V. VALE
I don't know what ad-hoc means.

That we ought to be spontaneous and react to the situation.

V. VALE
Of course you do! You have to be fully present. Like if you're talking to me, I'm not spacing out. I'm trying not to. I'm talking back to you. I'm not thinking about a million other things. Well, I am. But I'm not. All of us try to be fully present while another real life person is here talking to us.

Some do but others don't.

V. VALE
Fuck them.

WHY   SO   SERIOUS?
A Plague of Humour Deficiency

Do you ever get the feeling we're taking this all too seriously? In creativity-as-work, to make anything that pokes fun at itself is taboo. The desperation to come across as competent and professional has become the branded world of blah-blah-blah. Non-stop self-promotion has trumped the riskier likeability of self-deprecation (aka being able to laugh at yourself). Creative output needs to maintain this veneer, a requirement that automatically rules out any ideas that are self-effacing. Suggesting something may be less-than-perfect is not permitted. Instead, projects are treated as life or death because to admit 'it's only marketing' is still the truth which we cannot speak of.

A creative workplace may be a hoot and the creative process itself playful, but the resulting creation must be serious. Is this because we are made to feel lucky to be making a living this way, so out of respect we mustn't have too much fun? What happened to scare us away from making lighter work that could read as frivolous? Does the boss live in an ad era of the past when imposing marble and heavy rhyming slogans were in vogue? Or are we simply too depressed and burnt out by life to find value in the weird, the fun, the surreal?

LIGHTEN   UP,
IT'S   ONLY   MARKETING!

The rise of that intense and all-abiding 'Digital is King' belief system in the creative industries has corresponded with its increasing seriousness. Every brand needed a crusade, a cause (in other words, a pretend ethical reason to exist beyond making money). To be funny is to make light of the important issues of the 21st century. Duh. Who would dare laugh at our ongoing crises? In this context, flaws are not to be revealed because flaws = risk and risk must be minimised. Start digging back to a time before and you'll discover some infamous commercial creativity that poked fun at itself and used humour to its advantage.

Volkswagen Beetle's 'Ugly is Only Skin Deep' campaign
A big, bold, slogan over a frontal photograph of the car. As unapologetic as it gets.

Brewdog's 'Feedback' Staff Uniforms
'Overpriced pish. Fucking awful. What a company. Complete hipster paradise' – Ian Johnston, 2016.
'Garbage, overpriced and full of c^*%$. Cheeseboard is alright.' – Greg Husband, 2016
The beer brand prints the negative comments from online trolls onto the t-shirts worn by brewery bar staff with pride. Mega-likeable.

Listerine's 'The Taste You Hate; Twice A Day'
Who can't appreciate big ol' American copywriting when it is this wonderfully self-deprecating?

These three all engage in what comedians call 'The Pratfall Effect'. It's a method of poking fun at yourself based on the knowledge that admitting a weakness is more appealing to the audience. Exhibiting flaws can be endearing. For example, when a typically flawless TV presenter makes a mistake – stumbling over words or dropping their notes – their popularity increases. Being funny about flaws can increase brand appeal too. There is something trustworthy about being able to laugh at yourself. There is a certain attractiveness in imperfection. We find online reviews that give ratings of 4.2 or less out of 5 stars more trustworthy than those above.[‡1] Should we start looking at bringing a more light-hearted stance back into creative work for the same reason?

TRUST ME, I'M JOKING

Exhibiting imperfections, revealing weaknesses, and maintaining an ability to laugh at yourself all generate a sense of realness. It's attractive. None of this can be witnessed in the creative sector, where campaigns have only become slicker and more self-promotional. It comes as no surprise then, that distrust for brands and advertising has never been higher and that experts have described being in a 'trust crisis' since 2017.[‡2] This scepticism reaches its peak with those brands who soberly claim to be in it to 'change the world'.

Is anyone asking if seriousness is even likeable or if we want more pretend do-gooders in the world? As Leonie Roderick writes: 'Consumers are increasingly cynical of brands and advertising… with "arrogance" around brand purpose to blame.'[‡3] Can't say we disagree.

Humans are attracted to imperfection. We like imperfection because it feels real. Take our reactions to leadership. One of the most important traits a leader can demonstrate is vulnerability. We gravitate towards their fallibility since paradoxically, imperfection is not seen as a weakness but as a strength. When vulnerabilities are revealed, there has been a tangible demonstration of honesty. It earns trust. Trust is essential to loyalty (that thing incorrectly believed to be dead and coveted by every brand ever).

LESS   SERIOUS   =   VULNERABLE
VULNERABILITY → HONESTY → TRUST.

A SERIOUS TURN-OFF

How often do you go to a cultural space where the programming reads as earnestly important 'discourse' on the *ecology of the tacit* or a restaurant whose menu displays the latest in *bespoke mosses harkening back to the indigenous species of Northern Scandinavia?* Are these communications less attractive when they read as taking themselves too seriously?

WHY   SO   SERIOUS?

Creative work that is devoid of playful embraces of life, comes across as it. Output gets dull, dry, and forgettable, we lose all experimental potential for *I wonder what would happen if…* It kills any sense of wonder, transforming an attractive idea into a blip that goes unnoticed. Sure, there is a time and a place for serious discussion. But does all of life need to be a serious discussion? Endless debates over pressing matters, served with sides of hubris and bravado, mask deep concern about our uncertain times. They embody our current climate of outward unwavering success where everything is 'going great!' and nobody is saying otherwise. Instead, copy becomes hyperbolic, assuring us of certainty. Strained voices attempt to convey confidence. Where's the grit? Where's the humility? Where;s the humanness? All I can hear is Iggy and the Stooges crying 'No fun. My babe, no fun.' We miss seeing what would happen if we could only diminish the sense of self-importance. Swap the grimness and primness for a heightened *'why-so-serious?'*! When the mass desire is to be 'special' and distinct, this appears as a no-brainer way of standing out.

CYNIC   OR   CRITIC?
The   Difference   Between
Critical   Thinking and Cynicism

Hypnotised by online experiences – we're talking insta-entertainment, chatting, doing things on platforms, leisure surfing, researching, working, all of it – it becomes difficult to cultivate critical thinking. We are so zoomed in that we cannot get that wide-angle perspective, that big-picture-view that shows us how our work fits into our deeper intentions and desires. Key questions are cut out of the frame:

Why are we doing it like *this*?

What are the alternatives?

Is there something I would prefer?

How did I even get here?

Critical thinking is a critical matter. Are we asking why? Are we questioning the way things are done and refusing to accept 'because this is how everybody is doing it' as an answer? Do you think about alternatives and non-conformity? Do you feel compelled to defy that which does not seem right?

WHO   IS   ASKING   'WHY?'

These are all crucial elements to differentiating an automatic life from something more. Questions like these separate dull work from 'hold-up-wait-a-minute' work that is arresting and inspiring. With a critical approach to the everyday, one starts to challenge acceptability, and this is how we start to see (and make) change. In her address at 'Educate, Agitate, Organise!', Nadia Idle raises the subject of complicity and questions the default use of wristbands at events:

...I want to talk about... the silencing and policing of our minds which is going on, not just through overtly coercive tactics but by micro-aggressions and subliminal training of us into compliance, to keep us in line. Control of this sort only really

works if we are complicit in it. Take for example these wristbands we are wearing. Since when do we have to wear wristbands to participate in a university event? I really want to tear it off... myself, and the organisers, and all of you, are colluding in this mechanism of normalising tagging and the wearing of wristbands, to mark us somehow as official, or alternatively as if we are all collectively going to prison or something.[‡1]

THE OTHER 'C'

One of the words that threatens the cultivation of critical thinking is another 'c' word: cynicism. Cynicism masquerades as critical thinking and has become increasingly seductive in our present culture. It's seductive because it's easy. Cynicism puts nothing on the line. It's devoid of potency. It fault-finds from its despondent state, only to produce a resignation that seduces and then paralyses. Cynicism is a transparent gadget for self-protection. It is a stagnation that takes us nowhere.

When cynicism becomes the default language, playfulness and invention become impossible. Cynicism scours through a culture like bleach, wiping out millions of small, seedling ideas.

CAITLIN MORAN

WHAT'S THE DIFFERENCE?

*Critical thinking without hope is cynicism.
Hope without critical thinking is naiveté.*

MARIA POPOVA

Hope is the vital differentiator between cynicism and criticality. What separates the two is a radical belief that something more, something better, or something other is possible. It is that reactivation of hope which is the antidote to pernicious cynicism. It is the ingredient for progressive action at large.

Can critical thinking and hope coexist? They do not live at opposite ends of the psyche. The hope we're talking about is an active hope – one that lurches forth in action rather than sitting back and 'hoping for the best'. We don't need to be overnight optimists. We can stay empowered by negative thinking, by what Iggy Pop describes as the 'pure negative energy' that has fuelled his career. To think critically turns on the imagination of *doing things different* – that which naturally contains an element of hope, without conversion to the church of sunshine, roses, and morning affirmations.

RIDING IT OUT

Cynicism is for those who need instant gratification. Those with a sense of the world that has no nuance. It is for those who perceive life as simply as the internet often does, and respond accordingly: approval or outrage, confirmation or condemnation. Take protection and hone in on our capacities for critical thinking. Start to respond to your urgencies, those things that feel off inside, and give them some air time. Ask 'why?', even when it feels like no one else is. Be the one to voice a point aloud. Question the way things are being done. There are always alternatives. Create solidarity with those around you by seeing if they've noticed the same things. Converse over it. Strategise. Brainstorm. Dream.

If you're not feeling a situation, interrogate it. This is how we learn what's critical, and what's cynical. The cynical shuts down glimmering potentials, while the critical makes space for possibility. It scans the surroundings, honing in on what needs attention and interpretation. It locates the difference between what has been done, and what can be done.

RESPECT   IS   NOT   EARNT

Showing How We Expect To Be Treated

Many of us have been raised to want self-fulfilment from work and do all we can to attain it. Equating a life well lived with doing work connected to 'who we are' means that work becomes an expression and exploration of the self. By working on our job, we are simultaneously working on ourselves. How many 'Secrets To Success' have been written that divulge 'when you're working right, it shouldn't feel like working at all'?

Worker exploitation preys on the self-fulfilment narrative. When people connect themselves on a personal level to their work, they are likely to do more than what is required of them. This additional unpaid work – so the narrative goes – is not for the employer but for themselves. 'Bitter about getting home after 9pm each day? You shouldn't want to stop work that you love.'[1] Employers know all the tricks that leverage the individual's attachment of identity to paid work: 'this will be strong for your portfolio', 'we need the whole team together, we need you here', 'let's get this wrapped up, then we can move onto that great new project – I'd love to have you onboard for that too.'

To refuse working unpaid overtime is an impossibility for many. There are workplaces where not conforming to these exploitations comes with the real risk of being fired. In these circumstances, having money to survive is probably more important than defending an eight-hour sleep. Hey, there are people who love their job and dedicating time to it in any form – that's totally okay. But with the goal of providing strategies, here are some learnt insights that have been collected and tested with others.

IF   WE   DON'T   VALUE   OURSELVES AND   OUR   TIME, WHO WILL?

What we value and how we want to be treated come first. Respect is expected. We're not earning it. It can be demonstrated as a requirement. The idea that respect can come in time is crazy. Acknowledging the value of our time, our engagements outside the office, and all the needs that exist beyond paid work – which require no explanation to anybody else – is a base level respect to be expected from Day One. This is not something to be earnt or awarded in the future.

To have that sense of one's intrinsic worth which constitutes self-respect is potentially to have everything: the ability to discriminate, to love, and to remain indifferent.[‡2]

JOAN DIDION

Demonstration is a key word. Meekly asking for respect is often uneffective. It is not an object of hope labour.[§] We have to show how we live our lives with full expectation that this be respected by the paid work within it. We need to acknowledge the value our time holds and explain that to the outside by demonstration. Our behaviour is the strongest method we have to set up fair treatment. It is far more effective than words or discussion, where most people find it hard to not be dominated or bullied.

TO BEAT THEM AT THEIR OWN GAME

Half of seniority and 'being taken seriously' is how a person behaves and how that is perceived. In the contemporary West, this unfortunately means displaying 'hard' traits like confidence and assertiveness rather than 'soft' traits like kindness and emotionality. We can all picture the person in a leadership position who commands a room, or is on an international conference call, then glances at their watch, sees the time, and instantly changes the tone to wrap up because they have to go. It is an immediate assertion that their time is valuable. No space is given to entertain anything other than full respect.

Asserting respect as a requirement might mean a combination of performing to the codes of what 'respected people' do, and retaining the kindness that is respectful to others (the part that feels like being yourself in a place where there is more than enough dick-behaviour). From my own experience, mimicking the respected behaviour you

§ 'CREATIVE WORK HAS BEEN DEFINED AND CRITIQUED AS ESSENTIALLY FUTURE-ORIENTED 'HOPE LABOUR': UNDERPAID WORK EXECUTED IN THE PRESENT ON THE ASSUMPTION/SPECULATION OF FUTURE EMPLOYMENT.' ALACOVSKA, 2018.

see works. It doesn't matter how great your ideas and creations are, if you allow yourself to be taken advantage of they can potentially be overshadowed by a reputation for being overly appeasing. This aspect is especially relevant for women in the workplace, for whom the performance of 'masculine qualities' in exchange for respect is more hardcore. It is not right and it is a minefield – too soft and you're walked over, too hard and you're 'bitchy' and disliked. I worked with a (female) Chief Marketing Officer who dismissed fellow females who were quieter for being 'too invisible'. These people were discredited for not being loud or forward enough, and it impacted their opportunities at work since the Top Dog doubted them for it. This is an issue within workplaces that we need to be aware of.

MARKING THE BOUNDARIES

We can set boundaries of respect in our paid work. The earlier on the better. Marking respect requirements early on is more effective than trying to establish them later. Starting at a new position, taking on a new project, working with new people – all of these are ideal times to implement the refusal to go beyond what is agreed. 'Reasonable' requires definition, first to ourselves. What do you refuse? Outline it to your own definitions:

Working weekends?	YES OR NO
Continuing working at home when you leave the office?	YES OR NO
Loading work email onto your personal phone?	YES OR NO

Let your mind wander along previous situations of work and how those might have encroached upon your personal life. How did they get in? Identify the holes and seal them. One of my worst encroachments was starting at a new job and finding the signature in my work mail was set up to contain my personal phone number. I had never signed up for this and was never asked about it. It felt like an assault on the private information I had given my new employer in confidence. I removed it immediately and told them if a phone number was required they would have to provide me with one.

Although it may feel like it, it's not always necessary to provide detailed explanations of *why*. If you don't want to have work emails on your personal phone, no need to explain that to the whole team. Often a decision in action will say it for you. So many aspects of work communication have become normalised into our personal lives, like the expectation to be included in group chats and have those group chats on a personal phone. This normalisation is a problem and it erases the reality that it is an option, not a default. Gone is the polite question without any pressure: 'Do you want to be included in the group chat?' Instead it is assumed and then it is deemed antisocial to not be part. That chatting is labour. Are you interacting about work outside of working hours? Is it being remunerated? Is seeing work messages late at night affecting your sleep? If one wants to be included, ideally the interactions and time should be acknowledged as working and a phone should be provided. 'The will to work extreme schedules that encroach upon our emotional and biological needs for relationships care and sleep is what "Do What You Love" justifies in our contemporary culture of overwork.'[‡3]

What we are talking about is a matter of freedom, liberty, and how these situations impact not just our working lives – but our life lives. In his career advice for his field of journalism, George Monbiot highlights this differentiation:

...*My final piece of advice is this: when faced with the choice between engaging with reality or engaging with what Erich Fromm calls the 'necrophiliac' world of wealth and power, choose life, whatever the apparent costs may be. Your peers might at first look down on you: poor Nina, she's twenty-six and she still doesn't own a car. But those who have put wealth and power above life are living in the world of death, in which the living put their tombstones – their framed certificates signifying acceptance to that world – on their walls. Remember that even the editor of the Times, for all his income and prestige, is still a functionary, who must still take orders from his boss. He has less freedom than we do, and being the editor of the Times is as good as it gets.*[‡4]

Defining boundaries for ourselves is the easy part. Maintaining them is harder. It is the empowering differentiator between working for *them* and making work work for you. And ironically, it can be the differentiator between traditional career success or not. Respected workers get opportunities and are considered competent. Respect is part of standing out rather than trying to fit in. We are downgrading ourselves by allowing exploitation.

How we live our days is how we live our lives. Using daily decisions can demonstrate how we expect to be treated, and the respect we expect for our everyday lives. Remember, work and life should not be seamless. Keep the seams and make them visible.

SAD BUT TRUE,
PREVENTING   OVERWORK
IS PART OF THE JOB

≈

MY PERSONAL PHONE IS
NOT   A   COMPANY   TOOL

≈

GIVING ME A LAPTOP
IS NOT AN AUTO-
'NOW YOU WORK FROM HOME TOO'

WHAT'S   YOUR   SOLITUDE?
Aloneness   as   Alternative

When you read the word *solitude* what comes to mind? Being tucked away in a remote cabin? Going somewhere near a body of water all by yourself? Wandering an unfamiliar suburb without your headphones in? Or is it as simple as staring out a window, getting lost in your own thoughts?

Solitude is a vital element of our lives and an aspect of the creative process that cannot be compromised. It allows for those quieter thoughts and kernels of ideas to emerge in ways we might miss if we were submerged in our typical deluge of audiovisual inputs. It opens up the space and establishes the conditions for deep contemplation. By 'inputs' I mean anything that feeds us information, from listening to music to reading articles online. We are so used to these non-solitary situations that it's hard to notice that we are in them the majority of the time.

For us, it all started with the iPod. The invention of the iPod offered a constant stream of auditory entertainment, a form of ubiquitous media beyond anything we had experienced before. Its predecessors, the Walkman and Discman, had been too awkward to listen to at the bus stop or on a commute. Those were clunky devices, lugged out only on occasions like a long road trip. Those were the 90s. By the early 2000s, the bus stop was lined with plugged-in riders wearing white earphones. Now commuters could avoid all human interaction if they so desired, moving from A to B in an individualised bubble that looked and felt like recreational alone time.

Thanks to the iPod, we now had a means to listen to music 24/7. This constant stream changed the culture of listening on-the-go. Instead of devoted listening sessions at home, it was earphones-in from the moment one walked out the front door. Of course, the erosion of solitude by modernity is not new. 40 years ago it was the carphone that was the cause of disquiet, a device that introduced distraction into a space previously spent in thought. But what we are addressing here is the disappearance of solitude to a new degree over the course of our lifetime. This was the first time our solitude went beyond being momentarily interrupted. Now we had *continuous* distraction from our own mind on demand.

The iPod may have kicked off our new experience of non-stop input, but the arrival of the iPhone solidified it. Internet connection all day every day. It was now possible to eradicate the experience of solitude entirely from one's life. It kind of snuck up on us, right?

A SOLITUDE THAT IS NOT ISOLATION

There is a common misconception that solitude means physical separation from other people. That it is not true. Thinking like that only promotes individual isolation, which is not what we need more of, nor is it the point. Solitude is about what is going on inside our heads, not about the physical environment around us.

How do you get from connection to isolation? You end up isolated if you don't cultivate the capacity for solitude, the ability to be separate, to gather yourself.

Solitude is where you find yourself so that you can reach out to other people and form real attachments. When we don't have the capacity for solitude, we turn to other people in order to feel less anxious or in order to feel alive. When this happens, we're not able to appreciate who they are. It's as though we're using them as spare parts to support our fragile sense of self.[1]   SHERRY TURKLE

Solitude is a mind free from the input of media, stimulation, conversation, and distraction. Put simply, solitude is the important state of being alone with your thoughts. That means solitude can be found in a crowded train as much as it can in a wooden hut on a hill, as long as your mind is left to swim with its own ideas and feelings, its own desires and whims.

SOLITUDE IS A MIND
FREE   FROM   THE   INPUT
OF OTHER MINDS

QUIET DOESN'T EQUAL ALONE

Even in the most silent of moments, solitude can be compromised. It doesn't have to be another person that interrupts us. Even supposedly 'solitary' experiences – reading a book, listening to a podcast, or consuming content on a smartphone – can become experiences that shatter our quiet contemplation and rob us of sustained attention.

CARVE YOUR SOLITUDE

Are you deficient in alone time? Do you lack the mental pauses that keep you fit, agile, and energised? A life without these breaks is a life veering quickly towards burnout territory. Our time spent in solitude has become atrophied to the point of extinction. It is no exaggeration to state that most people in the West have solitude time very close to zero. As a result, everything suffers. Our insight is diminished, we have no time to balance our emotions, and we miss the calmness that can only be obtained away from the rush. And that's before we even address creative output! Do not underestimate this.

Distraction is usually a form of disguised lethargy, a way of emptying activity of any content, of stopping without really stopping. It is a form of non-work, but one that tends to induce a state of nervous exhaustion rather than rest.[+2]
JOSH COHEN

STRATEGIES: DEFINING SOLITUDE

It was not so long ago that situations of solitude were unavoidable. Imagine that. We were forced to be alone with our thoughts with no way out. Now we need to actively construct these situations for ourselves. It takes some preparation. Here's a start.

1. *Unlearn Hyper-Connected Culture*
It has been sold to us that being 'alone' sucks and 'the more connectivity, the better'. Not true. Aren't we all bored of Zuckerberg spewing on and on about his 'social mission – to make the world more open and connected'? Yawn. We know you made a distraction machine.

Get familiar with the idea that more connectivity is not better than less. Recalibrating life balance means adjusting to the fact that reflection has more weight than communication and prioritising it.

2. *Make A Plan*
We need to structure our solitude since it won't happen by chance. Designate specific times in the day and moments in the week to embark on adventures in solitude.

All of humanity's problems stem from man's inability to sit quietly in a room alone.[*3]

BLAISE PASCAL

3. *Walk, Walk, Walk*
Taking walks is one of the highest quality forms of solitude. No music, no audio entertainment. Just you, a pen, and paper. (It helps to expand our idea of walkable weather too. Cold days, wet days, all can be enjoyably walkable.)

4. *Thinking By Writing*
Writing is an exquisite mechanism to generate solitude. Deconstruct problems, organise thought, offer kindness to emotion, think expansively. Just as we are all creative, we are all writers. This may not be your usual go-to medium but when we visit it, the solitude that awaits shows the way.

5. *Leave Your Phone At Home*
Perhaps obvious but not having a phone on us removes the risk of temptation. Plan evenings without it. Make it a joint venture with friends. Arrange meeting points and discuss the fact you won't have phones to reassure yourselves it will be okay. Even leaving the house with our phones buried in a bag can be a simple deterrent to prevent its automatic use. The more you do this the more natural it will become. That urgent feeling to have your phone on you at all times will begin to seem overemphasised.

6. *Find Your Formula: Solitude and Companionship*
Every person has their own ideal blend of these two. You will soon discover yours and own it. Start exploring! For every hour you spend with others, how many hours do you need alone? Everyone's solitude looks different. What's yours?

ABUNDANT REWARDS

The rewards of solitude outweigh the effort required. Tenfold. At first boredom can be scary. So can that voice of guilt that torments our insides with the panic of *productivity*. But if you can struggle past these pressures and become an agent of solitude, you will see your manner change. This is your point of difference.

Company's okay, solitude is bliss.

TAME IMPALA

You know what's coming next: total radiant creativity. Original thought and effervescent ideas. To go offline provides us with the power to manifest all that lies within and gets little chance to come forth when distracted and drowned by inputs.

SOLITUDE RULES
ZOMBIE SCROLL DROOLS

FIND YOUR SOLITUDE

Find your solitude, your unique method of getting out what lies within. We are not here to march mindlessly in a line. Be in control of what you are doing. Question the social norms and default ways of life that the attention economy has imposed on us. Stay alert and question what is going on. After all, it is only with open eyes and critical minds that we can affect any change we hope to see. Now more than ever we need to make time for input-free solitude, the kind that lives alongside our automatic sociality. Solitude is as key to human thriving as our interpersonal connections. It's not one or the other – it's both! Dance between solitude and togetherness.§ Dance between solitude and stimulation. It's the dance of knowing your time is your choice.

§   WRITE THE HANDFUL OF EARTHQUAKES THAT HAVE COME TO YOU THROUGHOUT THIS READING. FIVE EASY BULLET POINTS OF WHAT YOU KNOW.

MAKING   SENSE

The	Language,	The	Problem,
And		The	Future

WHERE DO WE GO FROM HERE?

We lack the language to describe how we are feeling, the words to describe how technology shapes our lives. New terms have arisen: *attention economy, persuasive design, manipulative interfaces.* And we have started repurposing existing ones in new ways: *distraction, despair, loneliness.* Even the word 'offline' feels inadequate for the aspects of our lives we have been trying to explain.[§§] In April 2020, proponent for humane technology Tristan Harris released a statement that described this situation:

Living out our days through web browsers, news feeds, and Zoom calls has laid bare the industrialized world's reliance on technology to operate our coronavirus-affected society. Tech runs our businesses; maintains personal connections during shelter-in-place; and delivers our medicine, food, and banking. Isolated screen time shapes our mental health and hours worth of many children's lives now stuck at home.

The major tech platforms have become the social fabric by which we live and think. They increasingly control the digital infrastructure that now serves as the intermediary to human sense-making: They shape the information environment that helps us understand the pandemic, frame our elections, tune our children's education, and influence our mental health.

Just as the coronavirus forced our economy to suddenly deal with millions of unemployed and just as a private health industry is forced to deal with a public health crisis of historic proportions, so too are private tech platforms forced to adapt, with billions of people now unavoidably relying on them to make sense of the world.

Our reliance on their information is now a matter of life and death.[‡1]

As we try to build a new dictionary to make sense and name our terms, metaphors and analogies can help construct the bridge to get us there. Let's try to piece together a foundation of understanding, a basic ground that we can build on and move forth from. This is not the work of linguists or the job of those in the walls of Silicon Valley.

THE LANGUAGE

It doesn't take a Stanford degree to notice the dominant digital technologies in our lives are not humane. Mutating and applying coercion techniques and the psychologies of Las Vegas slot machines is not conducive to the wellbeing of the masses. One of the simplest lessons a child magician learns is that the mind is tricked by the things is doesn't see. Magic tricks can elude a person with a PhD as easily as they can capture a five-year-old. These are human traits that are open to manipulation on all levels, regardless of 'intelligence'. Because it's not about smarts, it's just smart illusion.

We can recognise we are all being extracted, which is different than having to say 'I am a victim of extraction'. In psychotherapy, patients are taught that rather than saying 'I am anxious' and identifying with it, they can reframe the anxiety into an object. This modifies 'I am anxious' into 'I am feeling anxious'. In our context, instead of saying 'I am the manipulated', we might say 'there is manipulation happening'. We are being extracted but we are not victims of extraction. 'We are victims' is a taught statement that creates feelings of helplessness. It is another tactic of these designs called 'learnt helplessness'.

At this moment a small group of companies run the entire human attention cycle. A handful of businesses hold the collective consciousness in their hands, but this is the same collective consciousness which can feel a potential overriding sense of togetherness. Rather than a reduced sense of power, perhaps we can find a counter oceanic feeling of togetherness. That ocean, just like the real oceans, is far more powerful than a room of wealthy humans.

THE PROBLEM

The handful of tech companies holding the collective attention hostage and producing psychological externalities like mass-narcissism, addiction, polarisation, mental health issues in children and adults, social comparison, and teen suicide, as well as the aforementioned learnt helplessness, have forged a system of power that is greater than the power of the individual. And just as extracting fossil fuel leads to climate change, extracting human attention from human beings leads to a social climate change. Never before has this been more apparent than during the Covid-19 lockdown, when we were glued to screens for hours a day.

This is a problem. And you cannot build political momentum if you don't have a common understanding of the problem, which is that the business model of these companies is inherently misaligned with the wellbeing of humanity. It's hard to see new problems arise when we are unfamiliar with the circumstances. Before the field of ergonomics was invented, it would have been strange to have somebody come up to you and say: 'Hey, sitting in a chair is bad for your back'. Sure, if you spent just 15 minutes a day desk-bound, there isn't a problem. But if the circumstances change and you are now sitting for eight hours a day in a non-ergonomic chair, you are going to notice. Parents were some of the first to notice the problem. Now their children were sitting behind that digital babysitter for eight hours, rather than the limited screen time of maybe one hour a day before, it suddenly begged the question: 'Is this really aligned with my kid's wellbeing?'.

They used to say a whale is worth more as oil than alive, and a tree is worth more as lumber than standing in some forest. Now the truth is that we are worth more to these companies distracted, than we are untethered. Since the rise of capitalism, there has always been a competition for our attention (think when the invention of the advertisement poster first appeared on Parisian streets), and there always will be. What are the ethics of all of this? We need a definition of what's on the table and what's not.

THE FUTURE

This definition and means of change need to come from multiple places. The first is policy. These companies won't make the right decision on their own. History has shown that they routinely prioritise growth and engagement over the public interest. The second is public pressure. This pressure needs to come from parents and children, from governments protecting their democracies, and from us. The 'us' is also the third link: the workers on the inside. This is not only the workers on the inside of tech companies but also the workers of the marketing-driven side of the model. Changing legislation is an achingly slow process. It takes years, if ever. But 2000 people on the inside saying 'enough' can have immediate impact.

As noted earlier in this book, writer and politician Upton Sinclair once said: 'It is difficult to get a man to understand something, when his salary depends on his not understanding it'. This defines exactly where we are at. Acting in public interest is a difficult road. However, it has become undeniable that the public utility infrastructure now includes players like Netflix and Facebook. This affects everyone, even if you are not on one of these platforms yourself. That is the impact of public utilities. Harris continues: 'If everybody else is on Facebook and they vote based upon it, that impacts your life. If everybody else is on YouTube watching anti-vaccine conspiracy theories and they don't vaccine their kids based upon it, that impacts your life. If you were part of an ethnic minority group in Myanmar, and you were affected by ethnic violence due to fake news amplified by Facebook, you didn't have to be on Facebook to be dead.'[2]

The pandemic gives us a chance to convert online lawlessness into humane and regenerative technology.

TRISTAN HARRIS

The goal now is to act for the public interest. Not retroactively, but proactively. To act on a civic tech that focuses more on *civic* than it does on tech. We can identify the problem and know that it is systemic. We can strategise about how to minimise its individual effects and how to work away from being complicit. But in a lawless environment, those who simply opt out cannot win. Because there is no simple opting-out. Here is a call to the public, the policy-makers, and the workers on the inside to see their power and rise up. For individuals, if you have a deep sense of connection to yourself, others, and nature, you don't need to seek fulfilment in digital technologies as much. However, it is going to take a deeper, harder commitment to our greater interest – that oceanic feeling of togetherness – to change what we are living with right now.

INTERLUDE
INTERLUDE
INTERLUDE
INTERLUDE
INTERLUDE
INTERLUDE
INTERLUDE
INTERLUDE

INTERLUDE

1. WHAT'S LESS CREATIVE THAN ASSUMED PREDICTABILITY?
Tell me when you find out.

2. UP FOR ANYTHING
This is the attitude to anti stay-home culture. Go to a concert before listening to the music online. Try a restaurant before reading the menu online or pre-checking photos of the plates. Experiment with life and see where the wind takes you.

3. TALK TO STRANGERS
Interact with people you don't know. It will change your life.

4. AVOID OPINION PIECES
Form your own opinion first, then discuss the topic with those around you, then perhaps see what other people are saying. Last step optional. The risk of exposing yourself to others' opinions is that you eradicate the chance for your own to form. Activate your own thoughts, ways, and connections. This is limiting input.

5. WHEN EVERYONE ELSE ZIGS…
Zag! Zag! Zag!

6. WEAR A WATCH
Rely on your phone as little as possible.

7. HOW TO CARE
Resisting increased individuation and isolation is self-care. Seeking and recognising collective joy is self-care. Maintaining friendships is self-care. Caring about others is self-care. Allowing yourself to be cared for is self-care. In a world where the self is central and the best selfie wins, we can still take care in how to care.

IV

8. ACTIVITIES VS. PASSIVITIES

Contemplate today's typical leisure time activities: watching TV, ordering in food, online shopping (Overnight delivery! Free returns!), interior decoration, perusing the bookstore... These 'activities' are what present time consumerism looks like. And while we speak of them as leisure-time activities, this gives them undue credit. These are not activities, they are more like passivities. We may feel active but in fact, just because we are doing something doesn't mean we are. All the activities above see us operating in the mode of 'having' which is a different mode of experience to that of 'being'. Can you think of an activity where you can actively be?

9. INTERESTS IS AN ACTIVE WORD

Perhaps this helps with finding an answer to the above. A note on the word 'interests'. Today when we talk about having interests (which is not possible, as an interest cannot be possessed) it misses the essence of what it means to be interested:
Interesse (Latin): 'To be in [or] among'
If it pulls an interest, be amongst it!

10. USE WORDS WITH PRIMALITY

Bend them. Make them yours. Find the combinations that you haven't seen or heard before.

11. 'GO OUT IN THE WORLD AND FUCK IT UP BEAUTIFULLY...

Horrify us with new ideas. Outrage outdated critics.
Use technology for transgression, not lazy social living.
Make me nervous.'

JOHN WATERS

12. CE N'EST PAS CONTENT.

‡ WELCOME

1. Igor Pantic. "Online social networking and mental health." *Cyberpsychology, behaviour and social networking.* vol. 17,10 (2014): 652-7.

‡ IT'S ALL MARKETING

1. Anna Wiener. "The Stories Silicon Valley Tells Itself in Order to Live: A Conversation with Anna Wiener." *Los Angeles Review of Books.* February 11, 2020. https://lareviewofbooks.org/article/the-stories-silicon-valley- tells-itself-in-order-to-live-a-conversation-with-anna-wiener/.

2. Cindy Milstein. "Reappropriate the Imagination!" *The Anarchist Library.* 2007. https://theanarchistlibrary.org/library/cindy-milstein-reappropriate-the-imagination.

3. Franco 'Bifo' Berardi, "When the World Is Depressed," in Barbora Kleinhamplová and Tereza Stejskalová (eds.) *Who Is An Artist?* Prague: Academy of Fine Arts, 2014. 31–44.

‡ OFFLINE ACTION AND INACTION

1. Don Slater. "Social Relationships and Identity On-line and Off-line," in Leah Lievrouw and Sonia Livingstone (eds.) *Handbook of New Media: Social Shaping and Consequences of ICTs.* London: Sage Publications, 2002. 533–543.

2. Bill Gibson. *The AudioPro Home Recording Course: A Comprehensive Multimedia Audio Recording Text.* Milwaukee: Hal Leonard Corporation, 1999.

3. Franco 'Bifo' Berardi. *Futurability: The Age of Impotence and the Horizon of Possibility.* Brooklyn: Verso Books, 2017.

4. Laboria Cuboniks. *The Xenofeminist Manifesto: A Politics for Alienation.* Brooklyn: Verso Books, 2018.

5. Franco 'Bifo' Berardi. *Futurability: The Age of Impotence and the Horizon of Possibility.* Brooklyn: Verso Books, 2017.

6. Franco 'Bifo' Berardi, "Desire, Pleasure, Senility, and Evolution." *e-flux journal,* no. 106 (February 2020). https://www.e-flux.com/journal/106/312516/desire-pleasure-senility-and-evolution/.

7. Cindy Milstein. "Reappropriate the Imagination!" *The Anarchist Library.* 2007. https://theanarchistlibrary.org/library/cindy-milstein-reappropriate-the-imagination.

8. Maaike Lauwaert, Francien van Westrenen, and Leo Reijnen. *Facing Value: Radical Perspectives From The Arts.* Amsterdam: Valiz, 2017.

9. Jan Ritsema. "A Liquid Revolution, for a Society Without Management, Money and Political Representation." *Academia.edu.* Last modified 2016. https://www.academia.edu/9824997/A_liquid_Revolution_for_a_society_without_management_money_and_po litical_representation.

10. Franco 'Bifo' Berardi. *Futurability: The Age of Impotence and the Horizon of Possibility.* Brooklyn: Verso Books, 2017.

‡ ANTI-TREND FORECASTS

1. Jin Li, "Assessing the Accuracy of Predictive Models for Numerical Data: Not r nor R2, Why Not? Then What?", *PLoS ONE* 12, no. 8 (August 24, 2017), https://doi.org/10.1371/journal.pone.0183250.

2. The Economist. "Can Data Predict Fashion Trends?." *The Economist.* July 27, 2017. https://www.economist.com/business/2017/07/27/can-data-predict-fashion-trends.

3. Geert Lovink. "The Data Prevention Manifesto by the Plumbing Birds." *The Institute of Network Cultures.* January 24, 2020. https://networkcultures.org/blog/2020/01/24/the-data-prevention-manifesto-by-the-plumbing-birds%E2%80%A8/.

4. Shoshana Zuboff. "You Are Now Remotely Controlled." *The New York Times.* January 25, 2020. http://nytimes.com/2020/01/24/opinion/sunday/surveillance-capitalism.html.

5. Douglas Rushkoff. "Critical Horizons: Douglas Rushkoff on Why Tech has Failed Humanity." Podcast audio. March 2019. https://soundcloud.com/thefuturelaboratory/critical-horizons-douglas-rushkoff.

6. NM Mashurov. "Double Trouble." *Real Life.* November 2019. https://reallifemag.com/double-trouble/.

7. Nadia Idle. "Collectivise Everything." May 9, 2017. https://notaloneintheworld.com/2017/05/07/collectivise- everything/.

‡ MILLENNIAL MELTDOWN

1. Pilita Clark. "Millennials: You Will Not Be Quite so Special in the 'Futr'." *Financial Times.* March 2018. https://www.ft.com/content/90b313a8-2857-11e8-b27e-cc62a39d57a0.

2. Akane Otani. "Your Lifetime Earnings Are Decided in the First 10 Years of Your Career." *Bloomberg News.* February 2015. https://www.bloomberg.com/news/articles/2015-02-09/your-lifetime-earnings-are-decided-in- the-first-10-years-of-your-career.

3. Julianne Harris. "This Is What Ageism Towards Millennials Looks Like." *Hello Giggles.* November 2016. https://hellogiggles.com/lifestyle/ageism-towards-millennials/.

4. Pilita Clark. "Millennials: You Will Not Be Quite so Special in the 'Futr'." *Financial Times.* March 2018. https://www.ft.com/content/90b313a8-2857-11e8-b27e-cc62a39d57a0.

5. The Economist. "America's elderly seem more screen-obsessed than the young." *The Economist*. August 2019. https://www.economist.com/graphic-detail/2019/08/14/americas-elderly-seem-more-screen-obsessed-than-the- young.
6. Wikipedia. "Demographic Profile". Accessed January 14, 2020. https://en.wikipedia.org/wiki/Demographic_profile.
7. Franco 'Bifo' Berardi. *Futurability: The Age of Impotence and the Horizon of Possibility*. Brooklyn: Verso Books, 2017.
8. United Nations. "Global Issues: Ageing." Accessed January 10, 2020. https://www.un.org/en/sections/issues- depth/ageing/.
9. Bob Hoffman. "Newsletter #107." March 25, 2018. http://createsend.com/t/d-20E5CF47D24035482540EF23F30FEDED.
10. Tanya Joseph. "Campaigns ignoring mature consumers are the folly of youth." *Marketing Week*. November 28, 2018. https://www.marketingweek.com/advertising-ignore-mature-consumers-folly/.

‡ FROM POSSESSION TO ACTIVITY

1. Erich Fromm. *The Art of Being*. New York: Open Road Integrated Media, 2013.
2. Ebiquity. "Re-evaluating Media." London: Radiocentre, 2018. https://www.radiocentre.org/re-evaluating- media/wp-content/uploads/2018/03/Ebiquity-Radiocentre-report-A4-web-singles-1.pdf.

‡ PURPOSE SMURPOSE

1. Patagonia. "Our Business and Climate Change." *Patagonia*. Accessed December 2019. https://www.patagonia.com.au/pages/our-business-and-climate-change.
2. JP Hanson. "The absurdity of brand purpose for the sake of brand purpose." *The Drum*. August 2018. https://www.thedrum.com/opinion/2018/08/31/the-absurdity-brand-purpose-the-sake-brand-purpose.
3. Erin Griffith. "Why Are Young People Pretending to Love Work?" *The New York Times*. January 26, 2019. https://www.nytimes.com/2019/01/26/business/against-hustle-culture-rise-and-grind-tgim.html.
4. JP Hanson. "The absurdity of brand purpose for the sake of brand purpose." *The Drum*. August 2018. https://www.thedrum.com/opinion/2018/08/31/the-absurdity-brand-purpose-the-sake-brand-purpose.
5. Ibid.
6. Ibid.

‡ INTERLUDE I

1. Rebecca Solnit. *Hope In The Dark: Untold Histories, Wild Possibilities*. Chicago, IL: Haymarket Books, 2016.

‡ WE'RE IN TOTE HELL

1. Katy Schneider and Lauren Levy. "The Coveted Tote Bags That Scream 'Status'?" *The Strategist*. February 2018. http://nymag.com/strategist/2018/02/best-tote-bags.html.

‡ THE CULT OF DIGITAL

1. Byung-Chul Han. *Psychopolitics: Neoliberalism and New Technologies of Power*. Brooklyn: Verso Books, 2017.
2. PR Week. "Read Marc Pritchard's Landmark Speech on Creating a 'new Media Supply Chain'." *PR Week*. April 12, 2019. https://www.prweek.com/article/1582002/read-marc-pritchards-landmark-speech-creating-new- media-supply-chain.
3. Louis Grenier. "Online Advertising Is Dead; Long Live Traditional Advertising?" Podcast audio. January 2018. https://www.everyonehatesmarketers.com/online-advertising-is-dead/.
4. Samuel Scott. "Marketers Who Prioritise Digital Advertising Have Delusions of Effectiveness." *The Drum*. March 19, 2018. https://www.thedrum.com/opinion/2018/03/19/marketers-who-prioritise-digital-advertising- have-delusions-effectiveness.
5. Leonie Roderick. "Will Other Brands Follow P&G's Lead and Cut Digital Ad Spend?" *Marketing Week*. August 3, 2017. https://www.marketingweek.com/brands-digital-pitfalls/.
6. Ebiquity. "Re-evaluating Media." London: Radiocentre, 2018. https://www.radiocentre.org/re-evaluating- media/wp-content/uploads/2018/03/Ebiquity-Radiocentre-report-A4-web-singles-1.pdf.
7. Ibid.
8. Paul Dughi. "Senior Marketing Execs: Virtually No Proof Social Media Ads Are Working." *Medium*. February 14, 2017. https://medium.com/digital-vault/senior-marketing-execs-virtually-no-proof-social-media-ads-are- working-df3e0d41ef92.
9. Anna Wiener. "The Stories Silicon Valley Tells Itself in Order to Live: A Conversation with Anna Wiener." *Los Angeles Review of Books*. February 11, 2020. https://lareviewofbooks.org/article/the-stories-silicon-valley- tells-itself-in-order-to-live-a-conversation-with-anna-wiener/.
10. Jeremy Merrill and Ariana Tobin. "Facebook Moves to Block Ad Transparency Tools - Including Ours." *ProPublica*. January 28, 2019. https://www.propublica.org/article/facebook-blocks-ad-transparency-tools.
11. Shengwu Li. "The Art Of Eyeball Harvesting: Shengwu Li On Online Advertising." *Logic Magazine*. January 2019. https://logicmag.io/play/shengwu-li-on-online-advertising/.
12. Ibid.
13. WNYC Studios. "Day 2: The Search For Your Identity." Podcast audio. February 7, 2017. https://www.wnycstudios.org/podcasts/notetoself/episodes/privacy-paradox-day-2-challenge.

14. Tony Romm. "Zuckerberg: Standing For Voice and Free Expression." *Washington Post.* October 17, 2019. https://www.washingtonpost.com/technology/2019/10/17/zuckerberg-standing-voice-free-expression/.

15. Shengwu Li. "The Art Of Eyeball Harvesting: Shengwu Li On Online Advertising." *Logic Magazine.* January 2019. https://www.logicmag.io/play/shengwu-li-on-online-advertising/

‡ **WHAT'S HOT AND WHAT'S NOT**
1. Kevin Simler. "Ads Don't Work That Way." *Melting Asphalt.* September 18, 2014. https://meltingasphalt.com/ads-dont-work-that-way/.
2. Jaron Lanier. "Six Reasons Why Social Media Is a Bummer." *The Observer,* May 27, 2018, https://www.theguardian.com/technology/2018/may/27/jaron-lanier-six-reasons-why-social-media-is-a-bummer.
3. Ed Keller. "Social Doesn't Just Mean Online." *Marketing Technology News, Trends & Insights.* September 19, 2017. https://www.martechadvisor.com/articles/social-media-marketing-2/social-doesnt-just-mean-online-heres-why-ignoring-offline-consumer-conversations-is-a-big-mistake/.
4. Samuel Scott. "Marketers Who Prioritise Digital Advertising Have Delusions of Effectiveness." *The Drum.* March 19, 2018. https://www.thedrum.com/opinion/2018/03/19/marketers-who-prioritise-digital-advertising- have-delusions-effectiveness.

‡ **OVER CONTENT CREATION**
1. Thomas Davenport and John Beck. *The Attention Economy.* Boston: Harvard Business Publishing, 2012, 17. 2 Jonathan Beller. "Paying Attention." *Cabinet Magazine,* (24). Winter 2006-2007. http://www.cabinetmagazine.org/issues/24/beller.php.
2. Jonathan Beller. "Paying Attention." *Cabinet Magazine,* (24). Winter 2006-2007. http://www.cabinetmagazine.org/issues/24/beller.php.
3. Jaron Lanier. "Six Reasons Why Social Media Is a Bummer." *The Observer,* May 27, 2018, https://www.theguardian.com/technology/2018/may/27/jaron-lanier-six-reasons-why-social-media-is-a-bummer.
4. Geert Lovink. *Sad by Design: On Platform Nihilism.* London: Pluto Press, 2019.
5. Nadia Idle. "25 things I learned in 2017." May 8, 2018. https://notaloneintheworld.com/2018/05/08/25-things- i-learned-in-2017/.
6. Jaron Lanier. "Six Reasons Why Social Media Is a Bummer." *The Observer,* May 27, 2018, https://www.theguardian.com/technology/2018/may/27/jaron-lanier-six-reasons-why-social-media-is-a-bummer.

‡ **SHOCK ME. PLEASE.**
1. Paul Cronin. Werner Herzog – *A Guide for the Perplexed: Conversations with Paul Cronin.* London: Faber & Faber, 2014.
2. *Donna Haraway: Story Telling For Earthly Survival.* Directed by Fabrizio Terranova. 2016. New York: Icarus Films, 2018.

‡ **TIRED OF PANEL TALKS**
1. Tereza Stejskalova. "Introduction." in *Who is an Artist?* Prague: Academy of Fine Arts, 2014.

‡ **EVERYONE IS BORED**
1. Josh Cohen. *Not Working: Why We Have to Stop.* London: Granta Books, 2019.
2. Ibid.
3. Ibid.

‡ **FAKE BUSY**
1. Silvio Lorusso. *Entreprecariat.* Eindhoven: Onomatopee, 2018.
2. Silvia Bellezza, Neeru Paharia, Anat Keinan. "Conspicuous Consumption of Time: When Busyness and Lack of Leisure Time Become a Status Symbol," *Journal of Consumer Research,* Volume 44, Issue 1, June 2017, 118-138.

‡ **LIMIT INPUT**
1. Stefan Higgins. "Crisis Mode." *Real Life.* November 7, 2019. https://reallifemag.com/crisis-mode/.
2. Friedrich Nietzsche. *Why I Am so Clever.* London: Penguin Classics, 2016.

‡ **THE 'JUST BECAUSE' METHOD**
1. V. Vale & A. Juno. "RE/Search Pranks." Volume 11, 1970. San Francisco: RE/Search Publications.

‡ **DESIRE & DISTRACTION**
1. Genesis Breyer P-Orridge. "Weaponized Pleasure." *Team Human.* Podcast audio. December 20, 2017. https://teamhuman.fm/2017/12/.
2. Nadia Idle. "25 things I learned in 2017." May 8, 2018. https://notaloneintheworld.com/2018/05/08/25-things- i-learned-in-2017/.
3. V. Vale. "Goals of Life with V.Vale." Lucifer Over LA. Podcast audio. December 11, 2017. https://www.nts.live/shows/lucifer-over-london/episodes/lucifer-over-la-goals-of-life-with-vvale-11th- december-2017.
4. The Carrotworkers' Collective. "What is work worth? About the counter-guide, free labour in the arts, and how to fight back." *FUSE Magazine.* October 2011. https://precariousworkersbrigade.tumblr.com/survivinginternships/.

5. Kodwo Eshun. "Everything was to be done. All the adventures are still there." *Telepolis.* July 10, 2000. https://www.heise.de/tp/features/Everything-was-to-be-done-All-the-adventures-are-still-there-3447386.html.

‡ **IMPOSTER NON-SYNDROME**
1. Nathalie Olah. "Impostor Syndrome?" *The Guardian.* October 16, 2019. http://theguardian.com/ 2019/oct/16/impostor-syndrome-class-unfairness.

‡ **AIM LOWER**
1. Douglas Hofstadter. *Gödel, Escher, Bach: An Eternal Golden Braid.* New York: Basic Books, 1979.
2. Oliver Burkeman. *HELP!: How to Become Slightly Happier and Get a Bit More Done.* New York: Random House, 2018.
3. Jon Bentley. "Programmimg Pearls," *Communications of the ACM* 28, no. 9 (1985): 896–901.
4. Makiko Yamada et al., "Superiority Illusion Arises from Resting-State Brain Networks Modulated by Dopamine," *Proceedings of the National Academy of Sciences* 110, no. 11 (2013): 4363–67.
5. Charles Jencks and Nathan Silver. *Adhocism: The Case for Improvisation.* Cambridge, MA: MIT Press, 2013.
6. Oliver Burkeman. *HELP!: How to Become Slightly Happier and Get a Bit More Done.* New York: Random House, 2018.
7. Nadia Idle. "Collectivise Everything." May 9, 2017. https://notaloneintheworld. com/2017/05/07/collectivise- everything/.

‡ **CONSCIOUSNESS-RAISING**
1. Anna Fisk. *Sex, Sin, and Our Selves: Encounters in Feminist Theology and Contemporary Women's Literature.* Eugene: Pickwick Publications, 2014.
2. The Institute for Precarious Consciousness. "Anxiety, affective struggle, and precarity consciousness-raising." Interface 6, no. 2 (November 2014), 271–300. http://www.interfacejournal.net/wordpress/wp- content/uploads/2015/01/Issue-6_2-IPC.pdf.
3. Ibid.
4. Nadia Idle. "Collectivise Everything." May 9, 2017. https://notaloneintheworld. com/2017/05/07/collectivise- everything/.
5. Miya Tokumitsu. "Tell Me It's Going to Be OK." *The Baffler.* October 3, 2018. https://thebaffler.com/salvos/tell-me-its-going-to-be-ok-tokumitsu.

‡ **ADHOCISM**
1. Charles Jencks and Nathan Silver. *Adhocism: The Case for Improvisation.* Cambridge, MA: MIT Press, 2013.
2. Richard Sennett. *The Craftsman.* London: Allen Lane, 2008.
3. Suri Fulton. *Thoughtless Acts.* Palo Alto, CA: IDEO, 2005.
4. Robert Waterman. *Adhocracy.* New York: W.W. Norton and Company, 1990.

‡ **WHY SO SERIOUS?**
1. Tom Collinger. "You Don't Want A 5-Star Review." *TechCrunch.* January 4, 2016. http://social.techcrunch.com/2016/01/03/you-dont-want-a-5-star-review/.
2. Leonie Roderick. "'Arrogance' around Brand Purpose Making Consumers Distrust Ads." *Marketing Week.* June 29, 2017. https://www.marketingweek.com/arrogance-brand-purpose-distrust-ads/.
3. Ibid.

‡ **CYNIC OR CRITIC?**
1. Nadia Idle. "Collectivise Everything." May 9, 2017. https://notaloneintheworld. com/2017/05/07/collectivise- everything/.

‡ **RESPECT IS NOT EARNT**
1. Miya Iokumitsu. *Do What You Love: And Other Lies About Success & Happiness.* New York: Regan Arts, 2015.
2. Joan Didion. "On Self-Respect," in *Slouching Towards Bethlehem: Essays.* New York: Open Road Media, 2017.
3. Miya Tokumitsu. *Do What You Love: And Other Lies About Success & Happiness.* New York: Regan Arts, 2015.
4. George Monbiot. "Career Advice." Monbiot. January 28, 2020. https://www.monbiot.com/career-advice/.

‡ **WHAT'S YOUR SOLITUDE?**
1. Sherry Turkle. Alone Together: *Why We Expect More from Technology and Less from Each Other.* London: Hachette UK, 2017.
2. Josh Cohen. *Not Working: Why We Have to Stop.* London: Granta Publications, 2019.
3. Blaise Pascal. *Pensées.* London: Penguin Classics, 1995.

‡ **MAKING SENSE**
1. "City Arts & Lectures presents Your Undivided Attention: Persuasive Technology," YouTube video, 47:40, posted by " City Arts & Lectures," April 30, 2020, https://www.youtube.com/watch?v=0TZKOuQLMfM.
2. Ibid.